KU-216-552

Chief Scottish Man

The Life and Ministry of Thomas Chalmers

Alexander (Sandy) Finlayson

Evangelical Press (EP Books), an imprint of 10Publishing
Unit C, Tomlinson Road, Leyland, PR25 2DY, England

www.epbooks.org
epbooks@10ofthose.com

© Alexander (Sandy) Finlayson 2020. All rights reserved.

First published 2021

British Library Cataloguing in Publication Data available

ISBN: 978-1-78397-297-5

Unless otherwise indicated, Scripture quotations in this publication are from the Authorized (King James) Version (AV), Crown copyright.

Cover image: © Henry Thomas Ryall, Rev. Thomas Chalmers, 1780–1847. Preacher and social reformer | National Galleries of Scotland.

This book provides a fresh and accessible summary of the life of one of Scotland's greatest sons—and a chief Scottish man! Sandy Finlayson honestly assesses the hugely significant influence Chalmers had on a very different Scotland from today—socially, economically, politically and spiritually—without descending into hagiography. The great Scottish church leader had a heart of iron with feet of clay! A refreshing reminder that even giants stumble! The book demonstrates well how the gospel which transformed Chalmers life and priorities should still fuel our vision. for contemporary Scotland. A nation that needs the church to be visionary, confident in the power of the Gospel to change hearts, but also communities and society. A church that empowers its people to serve and inspires in them a missionary heart and a radical social conscience. This book will introduce 'The Chief Scottish Man' to whole new audience who will be inspired and challenged by his life story, as I have been as I read it's pages.

Rev. Derek Lamont,

Minister, St. Columba's Free Church, Edinburgh

Who is the Christian leader from nineteenth-century Scotland whose ministry had the greatest impact? One could make a case for David Livingstone in the wider world, but inside Scotland itself the most likely candidate is undoubtedly Thomas Chalmers—a truly great preacher, denominational leader, and evangelical statesman. Sandy Finlayson has written a clear, judicious, and lively biography of Victorian Scotland's Chief Man. I learned from it, was inspired by it, and highly recommend it.

Dr. Timothy Larsen,

McManis Professor of Christian Thought, Wheaton

College,Wheaton, IL,and author of *A People of*

One Book: The Bible and the Victorians

This biography of Chalmers is written from a clear understanding of Chalmers' Reformed faith and with strong historical insights. Never was there a time when the life and thought of Thomas Chalmers was more needed than ours today. Chalmers' insistence on the theological integrity of the church and its commitment to biblical truth provides a necessary antidote for the wavering of many who claim to share Chalmers' historical lineage. His social and economic teaching provides an important balance to those who equate theological conservatism with social conservatism. Professor Finlayson writes clearly and with keen insight into why Chalmers has cast such a long shadow over succeeding generations.

Rev. Dr. A Donald MacLeod,

Research Professor of Church History,

Tyndale University College and Seminary, Toronto

Yet again, the Church of Jesus Christ, finds herself indebted to Professor Sandy Finlayson. Having previously written concerning the Founding Fathers of the Free Church of Scotland, Professor Finlayson, in the space of 11 chapters, now focuses our attention on the first among equals of these founders, Thomas Chalmers. He does so in a manner that not only informs the reader, but also evokes thanksgiving to God for a man like Chalmers, who like us all, had his flaws; yet at the same time, exposes the paucity of men of similar stature and influence in the 21st Century Church. The first chapter, which gives an overview of Scottish Church history since the Reformation, is itself, worth the price of the book alone. We look forward, with eager anticipation, to other writings from the keyboard of Professor Finlayson.

Rev. D. Allan MacLeod,

Pastor, Evangelical Presbyterian Church, Toronto

Every serious church leader should be familiar with the towering figure of Thomas Chalmers: intellectual genius, compelling orator and the ecclesiastical giant who, in 1843, led the "Disruption" in which 450 ministers in the Church of Scotland separated themselves from the "Establishment" to form the Free Church of Scotland. Yet, at root,

Chalmers was a compassionate Scottish pastor who, moved with pity for hundreds of helpless families caught in the poverty trap, sought to bring about revolutionary social reform to desperate communities in the context of church and gospel. In this well researched and highly readable new biography, Sandy Finlayson will help to ensure that the legacy of Thomas Chalmers is maintained well into the future. A thoroughly enjoyable and inspiring read.

Rev. Iver Martin,

Principal, Edinburgh Theological Seminary,

The Mound, Edinburgh

Thomas Chalmers was a colossal figure who deserves to be far more widely known and studied today. He was in the first-rank of preachers in his era; his social reform and political thought exercised a tremendous influence on Scotland; and his place as a professor and churchman put him at the center of Scottish Church History during one of its most significant eras. If Chalmers is unfamiliar to you, then this is the place to start. Sandy Finlayson's biography is clearly written and accessible, while interacting with the best scholarship and primary sources. It shows an appreciation for the personality and accomplishments of its subject, but it never slips into hagiography or holds back on legitimate criticism. This is a book worthy of your time, and Chalmers is a man worthy of your appreciation.

Rev. Dr. Jonathan L. Master,

President, Greenville Presbyterian Theological Seminary

While little known today, Thomas Chalmers was a colossus in the mid-nineteenth century, of such stature that even Karl Marx felt the need to name and shame him in *Das Kapital*. A scholar, a philosopher, an economist but, above all a churchman and a Christian, his was a life lived to the full. Here, Sandy Finlayson continues his project of bringing nineteenth century Free Church divines to life for a new day and a new audience by focusing on the greatest of them all. Clear, concise and accessible.

Rev. Dr. Carl R. Trueman,
Professor of Biblical and Religious Studies,
Grove City College, Grove City, PA

This revised and expanded portrait of one of Scotland's chief men is written with the best qualities of a sympathetic biography, and readers will find it responsible, engaging, and instructive. Finlayson writes a book which every Christian should read, for it introduces us to a man with godly ambition, a reformer's vision, and a few of the faults sometimes found in great men. The first two we sorely need in the church today. The last we must learn to forgive in others, and see in ourselves, and this life and study of Thomas Chalmers well help us to that end.

Rev. Dr. Chad Van Dixhoorn,
Professor of Church History, Westminster Theological Seminary,
Philadelphia, PA

Don't let the compactness of Professor Finlayson's work on Chalmers deceive you. It is chock full of useful information on the subjects of shepherding strategy, preaching, church history, church and state, mercy ministry, church planting, and pastoral leadership. All of this comes in the context of the life story of a faithful servant of Christ. This volume will inform, encourage, and equip you to grow in your effectiveness as a shepherd of God's flock.

Rev. Dr. Timothy Witmer,
Emeritus Professor of Practical Theology,
Westminster Theological Seminary, Philadelphia, PA,
and author of *The Shepherd Leader*

For Rod, Mary Ann and Cathie

• Thomas Chalmers as a young man •

Contents

Introduction and Acknowledgements

In 2015 Evangelical Press published my brief biography of Thomas Chalmers in their Bitesize Biographies series. That short book surveyed the life and ministry of the Scottish church leader, pastor and public figure, and suggested a few areas where Chalmers still speaks to the twenty-first century. Given the scope of the project, there was much that could have been said that had to be left out.

This volume contains most of the material that appeared in the original book, but it has given me the opportunity to do some additional things. First, it has allowed me to add more details to the original narrative. Secondly, as a result of more reading and reflection on Chalmers, I have fleshed out my analysis of some areas of his life. Chalmers was a complex man who did much good, but at the same time he made mistakes, and it is my hope that this expanded volume will deal fairly with both his achievements and his failures. Lastly, this book contains an entirely new chapter that takes a closer look at his preaching and pastoral leadership.

A word of explanation about the title of the book is in order here. After Chalmers' death, his son-in-law, the Reverend William Hanna took up the task of writing Chalmers' life. Hanna used his diaries, letters and manuscripts and he also drew widely on other contemporary sources.[1] When the fourth and final volume was published in 1852 he sent a copy to Thomas Carlyle, the philosopher and social commentator. In acknowledging receipt of the book, Carlyle wrote this to Hanna:

> A few days ago, I received, and have now gone thro', with much interest and pleasure, your Fourth volume; for which, and for all your other kindnesses to me, accept many sincere thanks. This important work is now concluded; and I think we may safely say, is a piece of work well done on your part, and likely to be long useful to mankind ... It is not often that the world sees men like Thomas Chalmers; nor can the world afford to forget them, or in its most careless mood be willing to do it, when they do appear, in whatever guise that be. Probably the time is coming when it will be more apparent than it now is to everyone that here intrinsically was the chief Scottish man of his Time.[2]

The fact that Carlyle was not in sympathy with many of the things that Chalmers believed or did makes this testimony all the more remarkable. He had met Chalmers and recognized that he had done much for his church and his country. It is my hope that this volume will go some way to explain why it was that Carlyle paid this tribute to him.

There are a number of people I have to thank, who have made this book possible. I would like to begin by thanking Graham Hind of Evangelical Press, who approached me with the idea of revising and expanding the original

Bitesize Biography. He has been encouraging and supportive throughout the process.

I am grateful to the Board of Trustees of Westminster Theological Seminary for their generous allowance of a study leave in 2019, when the book was written. I am also very grateful to the staff of the Montgomery Library at Westminster: Donna Campbell, Robert McInnis and Donna Roof. Without their smooth running of the library in my absence, this book could not have been written.

I would also like to thank these friends who have read the manuscript and provided very helpful feedback: the Rev. Father Lawrence R. Farley and Mrs. Donna Farley, the Rev. Dr. Don and Mrs. Judy Macleod and Mr. Cris Simpson. Lastly, I would like to express my gratitude to my wife Linda Finlayson. Linda read and edited multiple drafts of the manuscript and more importantly, provided great encouragement and many cups of tea during the writing process. Her contribution has made the book much better than it otherwise would have been, but I remain solely responsible for the opinions expressed and for the blemishes that remain.

This book is affectionately dedicated to my brother Rod Finlayson, and my sisters Mary Ann Vandenberg and Cathie Morton. I have been greatly blessed by them, and they continue to be three of the most important people in my life.

Oreland, Pennsylvania,
1 July (Canada Day) 2019.

Chapter 1
Scotland in Transition

On Thursday 18 May 1843 the Rev. Dr. Thomas Chalmers walked out of St. Andrew's Church in Edinburgh, along with two hundred and two other ministers and elders. These men were leaving the Church of Scotland's General Assembly for the last time and within a few hours, Chalmers would be appointed as the first moderator of the newly constituted Free Church of Scotland. Ultimately, four hundred and seventy ministers and one hundred and ninety-two probationary ministers also aligned themselves with the Free Church. And, remarkably, all of the Church of Scotland's overseas missionaries joined the Free Church. At the local parish level, it has been estimated that forty per cent of the church's lay membership withdrew from the established church.

This event, which rocked the Scottish ecclesiastical scene, was the culmination of many years of struggle for the spiritual independence of the church, a struggle led by the Free Church's new moderator. Thomas Chalmers was certainly not the only leader, but without his vision, organizational skills, and his ability to mobilize opinion, it is probable that the Free Church would never have come into existence.

But, as we shall see, Chalmers was much more than a gifted leader in the church. He was that rare breed of scholar, teacher, pastor and public theologian. He was someone who not only had great intellectual gifts, but he also had a very practical impact on the lives of many people. As we survey his life in this book, we will see his various gifts put into practice. Despite his giftedness however, he was a far from perfect man, and so we need to learn from his failures as well as his successes.

Before looking at the details of Chalmers' life, we need to spend a few moments examining the times in which he lived. Even though he only lived for 67 years, this was a period of enormous change and transition. There were immense economic, social and political changes, but more importantly for us, this period saw significant developments within Scotland's churches. All of these developments would mean that Scotland could be said to have undergone revolutionary change during Chalmers' lifetime.

To begin with some socio-political data, at the time of Chalmers' birth in 1780, Scotland's population was approximately 1.5 million people. By the time of his death in 1847, the population had increased to nearly 2.8 million. To place this population growth in context, during the whole of the eighteenth century, Scotland's population had grown by less than 600,000.

On the world stage, the conflict with the American colonies was still ongoing at the time of Chalmers' birth. And if this was not enough, Great Britain was also at war with France. While the war with the French came to an end in 1783, the

French Revolution of 1789 posed a real threat to the stability of Britain. There was genuine fear that the tide of revolution that was sweeping away the old order on the European continent would cross the English Channel and bring about similar revolutionary changes in Britain.

To put the political scene in context we need to remember that the crowns of Scotland and of England had been united in 1603 when James VI of Scotland inherited the crown of England upon the death of Queen Elizabeth I. While it was a moment of triumph for the Scots to see James Stuart crowned King of England, the next one hundred years saw periods of intense drama and conflict. The rise and fall of the fortunes of the Stuart dynasty, which included the English Civil War and the Glorious Revolution of 1688, would have wide reaching ramifications for English-Scottish relations.

When Queen Anne died without an heir in 1714, England, and eventually Scotland, turned to a German royal house for their next monarch. There was reluctance on the part of some Scots to embrace the House of Hanover in the person of George I. Despite justifiable suspicions regarding the Roman Catholic sympathies of some of the Stuart monarchs and their families, they were nonetheless seen as a Scottish dynasty and as a result, there was considerable sympathy for their ongoing claims to the throne. James II, who had been deposed during the Glorious Revolution of 1688, never gave up his claim and his heir, Bonnie Prince Charlie, would continue the campaign. Persistent risings were finally suppressed at the decisive and brutal Battle of Culloden in 1746.

The Acts of Union of 1707[1] which formally united the Scottish and English Parliaments were intended to emphasize the common aspirations of a United Britain. These acts merged the parliaments of the two nations and established the Kingdom of Great Britain. Scotland now had free trade with England and her colonies. As Britain's empire expanded the Scots played a great part in its development.

The end of the eighteenth century has been called "Scotland's most creative period": David Hume won world fame in philosophy and history, Adam Smith in political economy, and Robert Burns in poetry. In the next generation, Sir Walter Scott made the land, people and history of Scotland known throughout the world and Scottish inventors made discoveries that helped to advance the industrial revolution. Also, during this period, the Scots played a major role in establishing the colonies in Canada, Australia and New Zealand.

The single largest societal change that took place during the lifetime of Thomas Chalmers was the advance of the industrial revolution. The chief form of employment moved from the fields to the factories and, with this growth of manufacturing, came a major shift in population from rural areas to the cities. It was not that the agricultural sector entirely collapsed during this period, but the industrial sector was on a massive growth curve. Scotland's two largest cities, Glasgow and Edinburgh, saw significant growth. In 1801 the populations of Glasgow and Edinburgh were 77,000 and 83,000. Just fifty years later they were 345,000 and 194,000 respectively.

While this rapid growth was an indication of growing prosperity for some, there were also serious problems facing Scotland. Along with increased wealth generated by the manufacturing industries came massive social problems. While factory work could provide decent enough wages for some, this often came at significant social cost. Working conditions were frequently difficult and often dangerous. The health and safety laws that most of us take for granted were nowhere present. Many people were required to work seventeen hours a day and then lived the rest of the time in cramped, unhygienic and squalid conditions. While the British economy could be seen to be very prosperous the question was being asked, at what human cost? Crime in the cities was on the rise and there were serious issues caused by easy access to alcohol. One scholar has summarized the changes taking place in this way:

> The growing specialization in agriculture and the advent of steam-powered machinery helped to localize labor in towns, creating physical problems in health, housing and sanitation. The economic problems of growth, cyclical fluctuation and structural unemployment ensured that the transformation would not be easy. The emergence of new social groupings in new locations led to divisions between classes which were not simply physical but moral and cultural too.[2]

Immigration was another factor that was changing Scottish society in this period. Cheap labour, particularly from Ireland, flocked to the cities looking for work. Families separated from their roots and social structures added to the challenges being faced by Scotland's cities. In light of all of this it may be asked, how well was the church responding to the rapid change?

At the end of the eighteenth century Britain as a whole and Scotland in particular had a largely church-going population. In England, the Church of England commanded the largest share of those who attended church, although non-conformist

Protestants and Roman Catholic populations were on the increase.[3] In Scotland, the Church of Scotland, which was Presbyterian in polity, commanded the largest share of the populace by a wide margin.

The Church of Scotland was made the established church by the Act of Settlement in 1689. This was achieved after significant struggle and at no small loss of life. The Covenanters had valiantly resisted various attempts on the part of the House of Stuart to impose the Episcopalian form of church government and the *Book of Common Prayer* upon them. But even though Episcopalian government and worship had been successfully resisted, there were still problems, and one of the biggest issues had to do with how parish ministers were appointed. This issue would loom large during the lifetime of Thomas Chalmers.

Even before the Protestant Reformation, some landowners had taken upon themselves the right to appoint the local parish priest. New ideas of church government that emerged after the Reformation included attempts to do away with this system of patronage and replace it with a system whereby members of congregations could elect their own pastors. However, landowners, Protestant and Roman Catholic alike, were unwilling to give up their long-standing rights. During the seventeenth and eighteenth centuries a number of pieces of legislation were passed by Parliament that attempted to settle these thorny issues. Conflicting laws first abolished patronage in 1649, then re-established it in 1662, abolished it again in 1690, only to have it re-established in the Patronage Act of 1712. Thus, by the end of the eighteenth and early part of the nineteenth centuries there was both confusion and conflict within the Church of Scotland regarding who had the right to call ministers.

By the end of the eighteenth century the Church of Scotland had suffered from a number of relatively small secessions caused in part by differing views on the church's relation to the state. The secession churches objected to the establishment principle which held that there is a link between the church of Christ and the state. This principle holds that both institutions have been created by God and it is their duty to support and further the work of the other. One implication of this view is that it is the duty of the state to provide financial support for the work of the church. At the same time, both the church and the state have their own duties to carry out and should not interfere in the distinct areas belonging to the other. So, for example, the power to maintain peace and order in society belongs to the state, while the administration of the sacraments and the carrying out of church discipline is the sole responsibility of the church.

Despite the victories achieved by those who had fought for religious freedoms after the Reformation and throughout the seventeenth century, it must be conceded that by the time of Chalmers' birth, the Church of Scotland was not in the healthiest of conditions. To be sure, the churches were reasonably full of people and the balance sheets were strong, but what of the churches' spiritual health?

The Church of Scotland in this period was largely divided into two groups. While generalizing about these two groups can lead to over-simplification, a few important characteristics can be noted. On the one side were the "moderates" for whom the work of the church was more about appearing respectable in the eyes of the leaders of society, than it was about preaching the gospel. For the moderates, the church was as much a social entity within the society as it was a spiritual one. Their first principle was that the church must accept the principle of patronage and not give in to those who were increasingly demanding that individual congregations must have a greater role in calling their ministers. To be fair, there were those who believed that allowing patrons to select parish ministers was the best guarantee of having a well-educated and qualified clergy. They argued that the average man in the pew didn't have sufficient education and background to make a wise choice when calling a minister. To modern ears, this sounds paternalistic but at the end of the eighteenth century it was a view that was considered plausible.

The moderates in the Church of Scotland also included those who, if they had their way, would have reduced the church's subscription to the Westminster Confession of Faith, which all ministers, elders and deacons were required to agree to before they could assume their offices. In addition, the moderate party was accused of having insufficient zeal for reaching out to the unchurched or for applying the gospel to the increasing social problems that Scotland was facing. This would become particularly evident in the cities where there was reluctance to set up new parishes and open new churches to provide for the growing population who desperately needed spiritual counsel and support. With respect to the preaching of the moderates, Thomas Chalmers is said to have described their sermons as being "like a winter's day, short and clear and cold. The brevity is good; the clarity is better; the coldness is fatal. Moonlight preaching ripens no harvest." While this assessment is probably not entirely fair, it does give a flavour of how the moderates were viewed.[4]

The other group within the church, who came to be known as the "evangelicals," were passionate about evangelism and outreach both in Scotland and to other parts of the world. They believed that the gospel could make a real difference in the lives of individuals and in the world. They were also committed to the belief that the church must be spiritually independent of the state and that it was the right of each congregation to select their own minister. But at the time of Chalmers' birth there was little evidence that these evangelicals were having much impact. The church needed change and revival if it was going to carry out the Great Commission.

Chapter 2
Early Life 1780-1803

Thomas Chalmers was born on St. Patrick's Day, 17 March 1780 in the small shipbuilding and fishing community of Anstruther Easter in Fife. The Chalmers family had been connected with the area since the beginning of the eighteenth century when his great- grandfather had become the minister in Elie, a small community six miles to the west. Thomas's father John ran the family business which included ship owning and the management of the local thread and dye works. By the beginning of the nineteenth century the family business was struggling. The movement of goods between Britain and France was being disrupted by the Napoleonic Wars and, instead of managing a diversified business, John Chalmers would finish his days as the proprietor of a small retail wool shop.

John Chalmers married Elizabeth Hall, who was the daughter of a prosperous local wine merchant, in 1771. Over the course of their forty-seven year marriage they produced fourteen children with all but one of them surviving into adulthood. Thomas was the sixth child and the fourth son.

Thomas's father was a devout Christian and was particularly concerned that his children learn and accept for themselves the tenets of the Christian faith. Like almost everyone in the community, the Chalmers family attended the local Church of Scotland parish church. Along with the preaching and teaching received from the parish minister, another formative influence for the Chalmers children was their father's large library of devotional books which was said to be the finest in the area. Both John and Elizabeth Chalmers were very active in the life of their community. John served both as a magistrate in Anstruther Easter and also served as Provost. Elizabeth too was active. devoting some of her time to working with the poor in the parish. When it is remembered that she gave birth to fourteen children, it is remarkable that she had any time to be involved in poor relief and other good works!

At the age of two Thomas was committed to the care of a nurse. This lady seems to have been a particularly unpleasant person. Rather than nurturing her young charge, she seems to have believed that stringent discipline was the only way to deal with the young boy. She had a lasting impact on Thomas and her memory would haunt him for the rest of his life.

When he was three, Thomas was sent to the local parish school, where he was remembered more for his physical strength and warm-heartedness than he was for academic attainment. The headmaster was nearly blind and also extremely authoritarian, and young Thomas spent more time trying to avoid punishments than he did learning. Despite his less than auspicious formal education, it became clear that when he wanted, he could be a very able student. Once he could read he began to explore his father's library where one of his favourite books was John Bunyan's *The Pilgrim's*

Progress, which had come to be regarded as a classic work and was widely read. Chalmers was also very fortunate that one of his uncles took an interest in him and began to instruct him in mathematics, which would become a lifelong interest for him. According to surviving reports from his youth, he seems to have set his heart on becoming a minister early in his life, although his motivation for this is unclear. Nonetheless, his choice of career was demonstrated by his pretending to be a minister and preaching to his school friends.

In 1791, at the remarkably early age of eleven, Thomas Chalmers left the parish school and began studies at nearby St. Andrews University. Even by the standards of his day, this was a very early age to begin university. His academic performance was less than spectacular for the first years of his course of studies. These two years were devoted to the study of arts and philosophy. In later life he would lament that he had not paid more attention to his studies and he particularly regretted that he had not acquired a better grasp of the classical languages. If he didn't acquire great linguistic abilities at this stage, he was fascinated by mathematics. In fact, he seems to have thought that it would be quite possible for him to support himself by being ordained as a minister and serving a parish, while devoting most of his intellectual powers to the study and teaching of mathematics.

In November of 1795, Thomas Chalmers began divinity studies. He appears to have been liked by his fellow students. He was athletically accomplished and enjoyed the company of his friends and particularly their "jocular banter." At the same time, some of his friends did note that he could be moody and was subject to periods of depression.

Although he was not particularly interested in the

theological lectures he heard, he became interested in the writings of the New England puritan preacher Jonathan Edwards. Edwards' book *The Freedom of the Will* had a profound impact on the young divinity student. It presented Chalmers with a worldview that he could relate to, one in which he could understand both God and man's place in the universe. Chalmers would later write that while he was by no means an evangelical at this stage of his life he spent:

> ... nearly a twelvemonth in a sort of mental Elysium, and the one idea that ministered to my soul and all its rapture was the magnificence of the Godhead, and the universal subordination of all things to the one great purpose for which he evolved and was supporting creation.[1]

Two other features of his divinity studies are worth noting. First, he found himself studying in an environment that predominantly reflected the interests of the moderate party within the Church of Scotland. There was not as much emphasis on Biblical Studies and Systematic Theology as one might expect and instead the emphasis was placed more on natural and moral theology. Many of the students who graduated from St. Andrews and who then went on to serve in parish ministry, viewed the work of the church as making people good and helping to keep society orderly. Obviously, this was not a vision of the church best suited for passionate evangelical preaching. It was also reflected in a lot of the sermons of the day where the emphasis was placed on how people should behave rather than on their relationship with Jesus Christ. This emphasis can be seen clearly in Chalmers' early sermons.

Secondly, Chalmers spent considerable time working on his rhetorical skills during this period. He was so successful at this that he began to attract hearers when it was known he was going to participate in college prayer meetings. The time he spent on honing his oratorical skills would serve him well in later life. While his written work seems somewhat ponderous to modern ears, he would come to be regarded as one of the best preachers and lecturers of his day.

In the spring of 1798, Thomas's father obtained a tutoring position for him with the Stevenson family who lived near Arbroath. In addition to providing him with a small income as well as a place to live, his father's intent had been to give him some exposure to the lifestyle of the landowners who dominated Scottish ecclesiastical and social life. While he was required to tutor the children of the family, he would also be continuing his theological education in his spare time. The young tutor seems to have taken a near instant dislike to his employers and complained regularly to his father about how hard he was made to work and how poorly he was treated. Not recognizing that his father had his best interests in mind, Chalmers left his post in November of 1798 and returned to St. Andrews to devote himself full time to finishing his theological studies. This episode points to a young man who had a very definite sense of his own importance and someone who expected to be treated with respect and deference that he had not really earned.

Thomas completed his theological studies in 1799, and then turned his attention to becoming a minister of the Church of Scotland. In order to do this, he had to find a presbytery that would be willing to license him to preach, and then a patron who would be willing to appoint him to a parish. Here he encountered a problem. The Church of Scotland's regulations for the appointment of ministers, required that a man be twenty-one before he could be licensed, called and appointed to a parish. There was, however, an escape clause which indicated that if a man was of "singular and rare qualities" this rule could be overlooked. Thomas, perhaps not surprisingly, felt that he was possessed of these singular and rare qualities and so applied to be considered for licensure even though he was only nineteen years old.

While he waited for the presbytery to decide on his case, his father instructed him to take up another tutoring position with a family in the Anstruther area. Thomas flatly refused on the grounds that the family was not important enough and that he needed a connection to a family who would be able to advance his ministerial prospects. Rather than doing what his father had asked, Thomas departed for Edinburgh which would become his principal residence for the next two years.

Despite his uncooperativeness Thomas's father was concerned to see his son settled and began to do what he could to advance his son's career in the church. John Chalmers was able to enlist the help of his cousin and friend John Adamson, who was the professor of Civil History at St. Andrews. With Anderson's intervention, Thomas was allowed to do both his oral exams and preach a trial sermon before the presbytery of St. Andrews. The presbytery was satisfied with both his examination and the sermon and thus, on 31 July 1799, Thomas Chalmers was licensed to preach the gospel.

Normally, when a man had been licensed to preach, the next step was that he would accept opportunities to preach within the presbytery that had licensed him. This would allow him to become better known to parish churches and to their patrons, who would be responsible for appointing him to serve a particular parish. But Thomas chose a different path.

Despite the fact that he received a number of offers to preach within the presbytery, he turned all of them down. Instead he left for England for a reunion with four of his brothers. He preached his first sermon at Chapel Lane Chapel in Wigan on 25 August 1799 and then preached the same sermon the following week in Liverpool. His brother James wrote to his father and told him that, while he was no expert, he believed that Thomas "would shine in the pulpit" in years to come.

November 1799 saw Thomas Chalmers in Edinburgh. He had gone there in pursuit of a tutoring job but was unsuccessful. His father, who had continued to provide him with financial support, asked him to return home where there was an opportunity for him to be appointed as the assistant minister in the parish of Logie, which was near St. Andrews. Thomas, however, refused his father's request, stating that he wanted to stay in Edinburgh, where he spent much of his time attending philosophy and mathematics lectures at the University of Edinburgh.

To his credit, John Chalmers continued to work tirelessly on his son's behalf. He did everything that he could to use his connections to procure an ecclesiastical appointment for his son. John believed that the best opportunity was to call upon his connections with Sir John Anstruther, a wealthy landowner who had the power to appoint ministers in six different parishes. But the Anstruther family proved to be unreliable much to the frustration of John Chalmers and the anger of Thomas.

Thomas's employment prospects did not improve until 1801 when the parish of Kilmany became vacant. Kilmany was a rural parish situated nine miles north-west of St. Andrews. The parish was made up of eight hundred people with an annual stipend for the minister of £200, which was a considerable sum for a recent graduate with no experience. Because it would take some time for the arrangements for his ordination and installation to be completed, Thomas agreed to serve as an assistant in the parish of Cavers. Although he agreed to take on this job, he did not undertake his duties with much zeal or enthusiasm. He wrote to his father that the work was quite easy and even indicated that the lack of work gave him opportunity to work on a series of mathematical lectures that he was going to deliver at St. Andrews University. This had been possible because he had managed to get himself appointed to an assistantship at the university. He carried out his church duties at Cavers in a rather half-hearted manner until September of 1802. At that point he resigned his church appointment and focussed all of his energies on his mathematics lectures at St. Andrews.

While Chalmers was considered an eloquent lecturer and his students liked him because he was also entertaining, the university authorities were unhappy with his performance. William Vilant, the Professor of Mathematics, complained that Chalmers was including as much social commentary as he was mathematics in his lectures and that the students were not learning the basic material that they should have. He became so concerned that he began to interfere in Chalmers' classes. Chalmers, in headstrong fashion, continued his fanciful lectures and then took the disastrous step of publicly questioning Vilant's integrity. Not surprisingly, his assistantship was terminated after just one session. And so, with his academic prospects curtailed, at least for the time being, Chalmers at the age of twenty-three was ordained and installed as the minister of Kilmany on 18 May 1803. He would spend the rest of his life in various forms of Christian service.

In surveying Thomas Chalmers' early life, we have seen a young man of considerable academic promise and giftedness, but also a man who was possessed of a highly developed sense of his own importance and giftedness. Despite the piety of his parents' home he seems to have understood very little of what it really meant to be a Christian. Rather than having a desire to preach the gospel and care for the needs of the people of his parish, he appeared to take up his ministerial duties as a career rather than a vocation. While this was the way in which his ministry in Kilmany began, a very real change would transform his life and his ministry in the next few years.

Chapter 3
Kilmany 1803–1815

Thomas Chalmers' first summer in the parish of Kilmany was a busy one. He wisely decided that he needed to get to know as many people as possible, and so he began an active programme of parish visitation. During his first few months in Kilmany he visited all of the one hundred and fifty families who were connected to the Church of Scotland, as well as conducting regular services and administering the sacrament of baptism as needed. However, as the summer passed, he concluded that he didn't really need to spend much time on caring for the people of his parish. Instead, he decided that his best career prospects lay in St. Andrews University and so he announced that he would begin lecturing again, even if he had to do it unofficially. His teaching gifts were such that he did attract students, but the university was unimpressed and sought to discourage these unofficial lectures.

Chalmers' father was deeply disturbed by his son's cavalier attitude to his ministerial duties and tried to persuade him that, since he was now a minister of the gospel, he should devote himself wholeheartedly to his ministerial labours.

Thomas dismissed his father's concerns saying that no minister found it necessary to devote all of his energies to his parish. During the winter of 1803, Thomas's commitment to his parish weakened even further. He actually moved out of the parish and took lodgings for the winter term eleven miles away in St. Andrews where he believed he would soon become an academic star at the university.

In fairness, we should note that Chalmers was by no means the only minister of the Church of Scotland who took on extra work. However, even by the somewhat relaxed standards of the day, it has to be conceded that he didn't take his parish work very seriously. He would return to the parish church to conduct and preach at the worship service on Sunday, but his preparation for preaching was minimal. Most weeks he prepared his sermons early on Sunday morning, would preach them and then return to St. Andrews on Monday morning.

His presbytery was also concerned about his ministerial work habits. At a presbytery meeting on 4 September 1804, Dr. Martin, a fellow minister, asked that the presbytery "insert in their minutes that ... Mr. Chalmers giving lectures ... is improper and ought to be discontinued."[1] This motion was carried. Chalmers reacted with anger. He wrote to the moderator of his presbytery daring him to send a delegation into his parish to determine if his people were suffering or were discontented with their minister. And then, displaying breathtaking contempt for the authority of the church, he concluded his letter with this statement:

> I will defy [Dr. Martin] to find a single individual who can substantiate the charge of culpable negligence against me. I will defy him to find a single individual who will say

that I have been outstripped by any of my predecessors
in the regularity of my ministerial attentions, or who
will say that he has discovered anything in my conduct
which betokened a contempt for religion or indifference
to the sacred interests ... To the last sigh of my heart I will
struggle for independence, and eye with proud disdain the
man who presumes to invade it.[2]

Despite his protestations of independence, Chalmers was
stung into doing something about his absenteeism. During
the winter of 1804 he actually spent five days a week in
his parish. While he was more physically present, his heart
was still elsewhere. Believing that the ministry provided
insufficient intellectual stimulation or public fame for
his talents, Chalmers continued to desire an academic
appointment.

Over the next two years he unsuccessfully campaigned
for vacant teaching posts at St. Andrews University and the
University of Edinburgh. His lack of success in achieving his
goals led him to remark that he was:

... one of those ill-fated beings whom the malignant touch
of ordination has condemned to a life of ignorance and
obscurity; a being who must ... drivel out the rest of his
days in insignificance.[3]

His failure to achieve his aspirations did not stop him from
informally teaching chemistry around the area and he did
attempt to link his chemistry demonstrations to Christianity.
Even though he could hardly claim to be living out the
message of the Christian gospel and was barely serving the
needs of his parishioners, he still felt able to say that the
Christian faith was true and could bring cheer to life and
hope for the future.

In April 1807, Chalmers temporarily left his parish and took up residence in London where he remained until July. He spent his time investigating the sights of the capital and learning as much as he could about the politics and economics of the city. His brother James, who was an accountant at a commercial firm in the city, told his father in a letter that Thomas had seen more of the city in three weeks than he had in three years. His lack of concern for his parishioners was displayed by his time in London, demonstrating how weak his commitment to the ministry was. In fact, it was little more than a means to the end of making him more prominent in a world that he believed should be taking more notice of him.

At this time, fashionable London, and indeed all of Britain, was focused on the struggles with Napoleonic France and, in particular, the impact that the war was having on the British economy. As Chalmers spoke with politicians and others in London he decided that he should devote himself to writing a book that would show the way forward if Britain should be cut off from continental commerce as a result of the conflict with France.

He worked on this project when he returned to Kilmany and by December of 1807 his *Enquiry into the Extent and Stability of National Resources* was ready for publication. In the book he argued that if British society was properly organized and regulated, then the economy could flourish based on internal production. His ideas assumed a largely agrarian population which could produce enough food and other materials which were needed to support basic human needs. It did not sufficiently come to grips with the forces of industrialization that were already beginning to permanently change Great Britain. The book also attempted to make the case that the British economy should support a country that could be confident in its own right on the world stage. He further suggested that the government should not allow unfettered industrial growth as that would be bad for the peace and stability of the population.

Another feature of the book was his argument that those who had great personal wealth and privilege should not be living their lives simply for their own pleasure, or at the expense of the less fortunate. He was not arguing for the abolition of society's structures or even its hierarchy, but he did argue that there should be much higher taxes levelled on those who could most afford to pay. Lastly the book argued that the individual worth or value of a person didn't depend on how much money people had, or how much property they owned, but rather on their contribution to the nation's ideals and aims.

The fact that he didn't have a publisher for his book didn't discourage him. At his own expense he had five hundred copies printed and sent copies to all those he deemed to be shapers of public opinion. Then he waited for the reviews. Sadly, most of them were uncomplimentary. One particularly harsh review commented that the author's "command of language is probably a fatal snare … for as he seems to be at no loss for words, he is led to mistake fluency of expression for fertility of thought."[4]

While this and other reviews stung him, what hurt the most was that the decision makers and influencers of public opinion he most hoped to impress largely ignored his work. While it's tempting to dismiss this book as a mere footnote to his life, it is important to note that the book did display real concern for the welfare of the society in general, and particularly for those who were less fortunate. This as we shall see, would later become a major focus of Chalmers' life and ministry.

Somewhat chastened by this unsuccessful publishing venture, Chalmers returned to his parish work. Over the next couple of years, he remained in the parish more and seemed to have finally accepted the fact that he was not going to achieve great academic notoriety. One project that kept his attention at this time was the construction of a new manse for him to live in as the old one was in a seriously dilapidated condition.

His next campaign was to try to persuade the Church of Scotland that it should work harder to have ministerial stipends increased. These stipends were set by act of Parliament and it was up to the Church of Scotland to make the case that increases were needed. In 1809, he presented a petition on behalf of the presbytery of Cupar to the General Assembly of the Church of Scotland arguing for this increase. He stated that ministers' stipends should be increased so that they could "maintain their rank in the community." He also suggested that politicians needed to recognize that ministers were a "powerful instrument of security against the disaffection of the people" as they sought to teach "the solid principles of virtue and patriotism."[5] His petition was not adopted by the Assembly, but his speech did serve to introduce him to the wider church.

Between 1809 and 1811 a series of events took place which dramatically changed Chalmers' life and ministry. First, in 1809, he came into contact with a number of young evangelicals in the Church of Scotland. One of these men, David Brewster, invited him to contribute a series of scientific

articles to the soon to be launched *Edinburgh Encyclopaedia*.
As the encyclopaedia developed, Chalmers was offered the
article on Christianity which he took on with considerable
enthusiasm. As he began this work he indicated that he would
do so by paying attention to the historical evidences for the
Christian faith and by giving serious attention to the writings
of the early Church Fathers.

Then in June 1809 Chalmers became very ill with
consumption. The disease had already killed his sister
Barbara and his brother George. He had been quite close
to his siblings and their deaths caused him to re-examine
the course of his own life. During the summer his own
condition worsened, until there was very real concern for his
life. He was confined to a small cottage in Kilmany, where he
spent time in deep reflection. In a letter written to a friend
that summer, he stated that his own sickness was giving
him serious pause for thought about the priorities he had
established for himself. He also mentioned in the letter that
he had been reading *Thoughts on Religion* by Blaise Pascal,
the French mathematician, physicist, inventor and Christian
philosopher. Chalmers told his friend that the work was
written by:

> … a man who could stop short in the brilliant career of
> discovery, who could resign all the splendours of literary
> reputation, who could renounce without a sigh all the
> distinctions which are conferred upon genius, and resolve
> to devote every talent and every hour to the defence and
> illustration of the Gospel.[6]

This was a remarkable description of what it means to be
a Christian and it is clear that Chalmers wanted to emulate
Pascal's approach to the Christian life.

In April 1810 Chalmers' health improved slightly and he went to his family's home in Anstruther to continue his convalescence. While his health improved a little, he experienced a number of setbacks and tragedies in his personal life. First of all, his brief but passionate engagement to Anne Rankine came to an end. Their relationship appears to have been a stormy one, and it was Chalmers who initially doubted Anne's love for him. When he realized his error and he tried to win her back, she refused him. He was full of indignation, but later came to regret his outbursts of temper toward her. Adding to his distress, his sister Lucy died of consumption on 23 December 1810. As he attempted to deal with his grief, he began reading a book by William Wilberforce that had a profound impact upon him.

William Wilberforce was an English politician best known today for his leadership in the movement to end the slave trade. He began his political career in 1780, becoming an independent Member of Parliament. In 1785, he experienced an evangelical conversion, which resulted in major changes to his lifestyle and a lifelong concern for reform. In 1797, he published *A Practical View of the Prevailing Religious System of Professed Christians in the Higher and Middle Classes of This Country Contrasted With Real Christianity*. In it, he talked about the differences between true Christian faith and nominal religion. The book contained a mix of rational argument, personal testimony and ardent exhortation to the reader. The book proved to be very influential and was a bestseller as it sold 7,500 copies in just the first six months. As Chalmers read the book he discovered an understanding of the Christian faith that he had learned from his parents, but which he had forgotten in his search for fame. Chalmers was moved by passages like this one, where Wilberforce wrote that the Bible teaches

> ... that "of ourselves we can do nothing;" that "we are by nature children of wrath," and under the power of the evil spirit, our understandings being naturally dark, and our hearts averse from spiritual things; and we are directed to pray for the influence of the Holy Spirit to enlighten our understandings, to dissipate our prejudices, to purify our corrupt minds, and to renew us after the image of our heavenly Father. It is this influence which is represented as originally awakening us from slumber, as enlightening us in darkness, as "quickening us when dead," as "delivering us from the power of the devil," as drawing us to God, as "translating us into the kingdom of his dear Son," as "creating us anew in Christ Jesus," as "dwelling in us, and walking in us.[7]

Ten years later, Chalmers told his brother Alexander how influential this book had been.

> I had Wilberforce's *View* put into my hands and as I got on in reading it, [I] felt myself on the eve of a great revelation in all my opinions about Christianity ... I am now most thoroughly of the opinion, and it is an opinion founded on experience, that on the system of — Do this and live — no peace, and even no true and worthy obedience, can ever be attained. It is believe in the Lord Jesus Christ and, thou shalt be saved. When this belief enters the heart, joy and confidence enter along with it.[8]

Thomas Chalmers had come to realize that Christianity was not about following rules or moral principles. It was not about earning salvation. Rather it is a living faith in Jesus' death for sinners and his resurrection from the dead. In later life, he would say to his own students that "there were only two ways of being religious: one way is to try to put God in our debt; the other is simply to acknowledge the greatness of our debt to God."[9]

Chalmers' conversion had an instant and profound effect upon his parish work in Kilmany. As he returned to his duties following his illness, his priorities dramatically changed. Instead of viewing the pastoral ministry as a means to preferment and gaining recognition, he now saw that he was called to preach the gospel and serve his parishioners. His preaching took on a radically different tone. He was more passionate and the things that he emphasized changed. Instead of preaching moralism he began to call his people to repentance and faith in Christ. Attendance at services increased dramatically as his fame spread throughout and even beyond the confines of his parish. Some came out of curiosity, wanting to experience the new phenomenon. Others came out of their own feelings of spiritual concern. And still others came, wanting to hear the man that some were calling "mad" because of his passionate preaching. While exact numbers were not kept, based on parish revenue figures it has been estimated that regular attendance at services in Kilmany rose from less than seventy before his conversion, to nearly two hundred by 1814. Chalmers did note in his diary the numbers of tokens that were distributed at some communion services and there was a notable increase which indicated a greater participation in the sacrament of the Lord's Supper.[10]

While Chalmers had always had considerable oratorical skills, he now began to pay more attention to the needs of the people he was preaching to. Instead of writing his sermons at the last moment, he devoted much more time to studying and sermon preparation. Entries in his journals indicate just how widely he was reading. This reading list included parts of Calvin's *Institutes of the Christian Religion,* and many of the puritans and other evangelical authors. In addition, he read widely in contemporary literature, mathematics and science. What is also striking is his correspondence and contacts with people outside his own theological tradition. He would always be a man who was open to interaction with those that he didn't entirely agree with.

While his reading, and his letters, indicate that he embraced the basic understanding of reformed and evangelical theology, he never entirely systematized his theological thinking. He would always be nervous of theological systems and debates, which he feared might distract from the basic message of the Bible; but he was always clear that the sinner must turn to Christ in repentance and faith and then live a life of obedience and service. While it is true that Chalmers never wrote a systematic theology, this is not as surprising as it might seem, since the chief concerns of his ministry would always tend toward the practical outworking of the Christian life. After his death, some of his lectures were published as his *Institutes of Theology*, but these do not provide a conventional systematic theology as such.

As his fame spread, he accepted invitations to preach in other places and he always took care to preach in a way that would connect with his audience. By his own admission, he found it difficult to communicate with those who were less educated. Even though he believed he was not as effective communicating with farm workers and labourers, nevertheless one of the first people to be converted as a result of his preaching was a ploughman. Chalmers also now spent more time preparing and leading new communicants' classes, and the number of people who attended these classes steadily increased after Chalmers' own conversion. Chalmers also spent a lot more time and energy on doing pastoral work in his parish. The amount of visiting that he did increased and he was very enthusiastic about the catechizing of children. Not all of his energies however, were devoted to his own parish. He was beginning to have a much larger vision for the work of the church.

In March 1812 Chalmers founded the Kilmany Bible Society. The British and Foreign Bible Society had begun in 1804 with the express goal of making the Bible more accessible to people and encouraging the reading of Scripture. Soon these societies were being formed around Britain and Kilmany was no exception. Chalmers believed that the message of the Bible was important to the health of society, and he worked with people of diverse church backgrounds to bring this organization into being. He also wanted the local society to connect with other Bible Societies who had similar aims. He encouraged everyone within his own parish to support the work of the Bible Society even if they were only able to give a small amount of money. In so doing he taught his people that it wasn't just the wealthy or the minister who could have an impact on the growth of the church and the spread of the gospel. They too could help to spread the good news. His belief that the Bible should have the widest possible distribution led him to campaign for support for the Bible Society in other Church of Scotland parishes, which was not always well received by some of his ministerial colleagues. Chalmers' support for Bible Societies eventually evolved into his support for and advocacy of the Victorian Missionary Movement which would have an impact throughout the British Empire and beyond.

In August of 1812, Thomas's life underwent a significant
change when he married Grace Pratt, the daughter of an
army captain. She came from one of the wealthier families
in the parish and brought money to the marriage. Grace was
eleven years younger than Thomas and had spent a number
of years previously caring for one of her uncles. She had a
calm and practical personality and was able, over the course
of time, to temper some of her husband's more extravagant
and impulsive behaviours. She became known for her gifts of
hospitality and kindness as well as her ability to handle the
family's finances.

Chalmers' marriage was a happy one and Anne, the first
of their six daughters, was born on 5 May 1813. In Anne's
published letters and journals, we are told that Chalmers
welcomed each of his daughters, by giving them a "fanciful
name … according to the place of their birth. Anne's name
was the 'Fifeshire Fairy' or the Fair Maid of the Eden."[11]
Piecing together the details of Chalmers' family life presents
a picture of a happy home that valued music, literature and
poetry.

It is hardly surprising that Thomas's work in the parish of
Kilmany began to attract attention in the wider church. In
1813 he declined the opportunity of moving to London, but
in 1814 when he was asked to consider moving to Glasgow,
he found that harder to refuse. St. Mary's Tron Church in
Glasgow had a history of evangelical ministers and so when
the pulpit became vacant, Chalmers' name was put forward as
a candidate.

The elders of the Tron church were unanimous in their
desire to call him and after much soul searching he eventually
agreed that his name could be considered for election. The

decision was in the hands of the City Council of Glasgow, who were the legal patrons of the Tron Church. Vigorous campaigning took place, with Chalmers being the popular choice among the evangelical party. However, the moderates also had their candidate and they pressed the council to choose their man instead. In spite of this, on 25 November 1814 Chalmers was elected as the next minister of the Tron Church and on 2 January 1815 he officially accepted the call. A date for his installation was set for July of the same year. In his final sermon to the congregation of Kilmany Chalmers displayed his passion for the good news of the gospel and the reality of its impact on the life of Christians. Preaching from Colossians 2:6 "As ye have therefore received Christ Jesus the Lord, so walk ye in him" he said this:

> Nothing can be clearer from both the doctrine and the examples of the New Testament, than that a man changes the course of his life on his becoming in the true sense of the word, a Christian. There is no such thing as receiving Christ, and after that walking just as you were wont to do. Choose him … let him enter your hearts by faith, and let him dwell continually there.[12]

The minister who left Kilmany for the city in the summer of 1815 was a very different person than the one who had arrived there twelve years earlier. Instead of someone who was not really devoted to the work of the ministry, except as a means of gaining popularity and academic position, Thomas Chalmers was now firmly committed to his evangelical principles, the mission of the church and his desire to see the church make a difference in the world.

Chapter 4
The Tron Parish
Glasgow 1815–1819

In 1815 the city of Glasgow was divided into eight parishes, and each of these had a parish church that was responsible for providing for the care of the residents in that area. The Tron parish in central Glasgow had a long history. It had been established in 1484 and, after the Reformation, had become Presbyterian in 1592. The church building itself had been rebuilt in 1794 and seated about 1,300 people. Oddly enough the actual church building was located just outside the official parish boundary. This was not unheard of but it does indicate that the original concept of the parish system had broken down. Funding for the work of the parish, including paying the minister's stipend, came from pew rents, which were monies paid for the privilege of having an assigned seat in the church. At the time of Chalmers' installation, the total population of the parish was approximately 11,000 people, but nearly half of those were not members of the Church of Scotland. Some of these people attended other churches, while others didn't go to church at all because they either couldn't afford the pew rents or weren't interested in attending. The parish was a very poor one and it would not be long before the new minister would begin to realize just how big the task was that lay before him.

The people of the Tron parish were very pleased to have acquired their new minister and received him with genuine excitement. His evangelical preaching attracted more people, and he quickly became a favourite preacher in Glasgow. The conferring of the degree of Doctor of Divinity by the University of Glasgow on 21 February 1816 also increased Chalmers' popularity.

Chalmers' first challenge in his parish was that most of the people that came to hear him preach on any given Sunday did not actually live within the boundaries of the parish. His congregation at the Tron was drawn from people who lived in the surrounding area and who had been attracted to the church by the previous minister and his evangelical preaching. Because his congregation were paying pew rents which granted them the privilege of attending the church, some came to view the new minister as their property and expected that he would devote much of his time to visiting them and attending social functions.

Chalmers soon realized that this was a very different situation from the one he had experienced in Kilmany, where he was preaching to people who actually lived close to the church. In his first parish he had been able to devote almost as much time as he wanted to the work of the church which he saw as preaching, teaching and pastoral care. Now, he was expected to attend social functions and meetings on subjects that had little or nothing to do with the work of the

church. Such was Chalmers' frustration at these demands
that his letters contain statements of regret that he had ever
moved to the city. While there is a note of self-pity in some
of these letters, he managed to recover his equilibrium and
began to turn his attention to the people who lived within
the parish, but who were unable to attend worship services.
While he continued to preach to and teach the rent holders
who regularly filled the church, his focus became how he and
his congregation could care for those in need immediately
outside their walls.

His first step was to begin a systematic parish visitation.
Beginning in November of 1815 Chalmers, along with elders
from the church, began visiting the residents of the parish.
He spent whole days visiting as many as seventy families a
day and over the course of two years he was able to meet
most of his parishioners. Chalmers knew that he would not
get to know the people intimately, but he did take care to
keep statistics on each family and he made careful notes of
specific needs that he discovered. It is important to note that
his visits were not confined to those who had a connection
with the Church of Scotland. He also visited the families of
Dissenters (Protestants who did not belong to the national
church). More remarkably, he also visited the homes of
Roman Catholics. This was unusual at a time when there were
deep divides between Catholics and Protestants. The more
Chalmers visited, the more he came to recognize that the
regular Sunday ministry at the Tron Church could not meet
the needs of most of the people and, as a result, he began
to think about new ways to care for all of the people of his
parish.

The next thing that he did was to establish midweek
meetings in various parts of the parish. He invited those he

had visited to come to these meetings where he would preach and teach the basic concepts of the Christian faith. While these meetings would only touch a fraction of the parish, his visitation efforts and these special meetings did serve to make him much better known and respected in the area.

He soon recognized that the needs of the parish were so great that he could not make a difference on his own. As a result, he began to actively look for help from within his congregation. The Tron parish was divided into twenty-five districts or proportions and each of these districts was supposed to have an elder who was responsible for pastoral oversight and care. But when Chalmers was installed as minister, there were only eight elders. Eight men could not properly care for the 1,300 who regularly attended the church or the 11,000 outside the church. So, during his first year as minister Chalmers began to look for suitable candidates for the eldership.

Twelve younger men were elected to the office of elder and by December of 1816, Chalmers had trained and was ready to install the new elders. All of them were well-educated and had both the money and time necessary to devote themselves to the work of the church. At their ordination Chalmers told the new elders that under God it would be up to them to see that the parish system could be made to work in the context of a large city. While he conceded that the parish system had broken down in the cities of Scotland, it didn't have to remain that way.

He then went on to give them a threefold charge. First it was their duty to teach the good news about Jesus through regular visitation. Second, they were to be proactive in looking for those who needed material assistance from the church. Families should be encouraged to help themselves and, wherever possible, care for their own; but the elders were to make sure that people who genuinely needed it would be provided with support. Thirdly the elders were to encourage others who regularly attended the Tron to become actively involved in parish life. His hope was to mobilize the resources of a middle-class congregation to give of their time, talent and treasure to care for the less fortunate. Chalmers was no revolutionary and wasn't interested in breaking down class distinctions, but he did believe that social harmony was possible and that it was part of the mission of the church to encourage this harmony within communities. Some have argued that Chalmers' vision of society was outmoded and oppressive to the poor, but he cannot be accused of not caring for spiritual and physical needs of those outside of the walls of his church. Not all needs were met but the mobilized and reinvigorated eldership did make a difference. People still fell between the cracks, but the Tron parish and the city of Glasgow were both much better places as a result of Chalmers' initiatives.

Sabbath or Sunday Schools were another initiative that Chalmers used to reach out to his parish. It is important to note here that Chalmers did not invent the Sunday School Movement but he did adapt it to meet local needs. One of the things that he noticed during his visitations was that many people had little or no education and that illiteracy rates were very high. He wanted to raise literacy levels to better equip people to lead more productive lives and so that they could more fully understand the gospel.

What was novel about Chalmers' approach to Sunday Schools was that he took the parish model of oversight and pastoral care and applied this to the Sunday Schools. He then looked within his own congregation for able men who were willing to teach. Because his congregation was largely comprised of middle class, well-educated people he had a good pool of talent to draw from. He drew on the talents of men like David Stow (1793–1864) and William Collins (1789–1853) who were already involved in education. Collins had been one of the men involved in attracting Chalmers to Glasgow and would eventually become the publisher of most of Chalmers' books when he established his own publishing firm. David Stow was the founder of the Glasgow Education Society, which had had some success in raising literacy levels in Glasgow. A Sunday School society was established in December of 1816 with only four teachers. By the time Chalmers left the parish three years later, there were over forty teachers and forty-seven schools, which made up almost half the total number of schools in all of Glasgow. In addition to providing for both basic literacy and the religious education of many young people, Chalmers' Sunday School scheme had another major benefit. Some of the teachers, who previously had been unaware of the difficult living situations of many Glasgow citizens, learned of the state of the inner city and were moved to devote significant efforts to improving the conditions. Also, a number of young men would ultimately decide to go into the ministries of the Church of Scotland, and later the Free Church, as a result of their experience in the Tron parish's Sunday School work. Another sign of the success of this endeavor was that the organization of the schools would be replicated in other parishes in Scotland.

While this part of Chalmers' parish ministry was a success, it was not always well received. Some in his parish objected to the fact that their minister was spending too much time on this, rather than visiting them or attending their social gatherings. They took the view that they were paying his stipend through their pew rents, so they deserved more say in how their minister spent his time. Chalmers did not take well to this criticism. He castigated his congregation for their being so inward-looking, and in January of 1817, he announced that he was considering a call to another parish in Stirling. When this news broke his friends and allies within the congregation mounted a campaign which persuaded him to stay, for at least a while longer. While many of those who opposed him ultimately left to worship in other parishes, they were soon replaced by other people who were attracted to the Tron because of Chalmers' preaching.

During his time in the Tron parish, Chalmers preached a number of sermons which cemented his reputation as one of the great evangelical preachers of his day. Even though Chalmers typically read his sermons from manuscript he, nevertheless, was able to lift the words off the page in a way that captivated his audiences. We will have more to say about Chalmers' approach to regular weekly preaching in a later chapter, but it is important to pause here to take note of the series that made his reputation as one of the great preachers of the Victorian era, particularly in Scotland.

The sermons that most captured the public's imagination were those that came to be known as the *Astronomical Discourses,* which were preached between November 1815 and October 1816. These sermons were part of a series that were intended for the business and professional classes who worked in the city. Each of the Church of Scotland clergyman in the city took turns delivering the sermons, although they were all delivered at the Tron parish church. The *Astronomical Discourses* made use of Chalmers' considerable scientific knowledge and his interest in natural philosophy. He demonstrated that the Christian faith had nothing to fear from modern science. He was also anxious to demonstrate that it was possible for a minister to be an evangelical and also have considerable knowledge of the worlds of philosophy and science.

These sermons were a response to society's growing awareness of the vastness of the universe and the claim that said that Christianity was implausible, especially the belief that the death of Christ on earth could somehow redeem humanity from sin. Rather than being daunted by the possibility of other populated worlds, Chalmers persuasively made the case that the death and resurrection of Christ were in fact God's way of bringing the whole universe back into relationship with God. There are certainly some flights of fancy in the *Discourses*, where Chalmers posits many populated worlds where there had been sin, and redemption as a result of the work of Christ; nonetheless his basic point is "the distinct and affirmative testimony of the Bible" and that its message can be trusted.[1]

What is most striking about the *Astronomical Discourses* isn't his answer to what is a hypothetical question, rather it is his warning that knowledge from science needs to be kept in proper perspective. Chalmers reminded his hearers that science should be appropriately modest. It was the purpose of science, he argued, to observe the natural and created orders and not to explain them. If one really wanted to understand and explain the world, the only infallible place where that knowledge could be found was in God's self-revelation in Scripture. Because it was there that God had revealed Himself as the creating and redeeming God who had laid down standards by which all should live. Chalmers further warned that if belief in God was replaced with a belief in science this would lead to each individual doing what was right in their own eyes, and becoming a law unto themselves. It was an important warning then and remains so now, nearly two hundred years later.

He concluded the last sermon with a powerful personal appeal. He stated that the knowledge of the goodness and graciousness of God as revealed in nature was insufficient for salvation. He also warned that everyone had to come to realize and accept who God is, acknowledge their sin, and then embrace redemption in Christ.

> Remember that the conflict is for each of you individually; and let this alarm you into watchfulness against the power of every temptation, and a cleaving dependence upon Him through whom alone you will be more than conquerors. Above all, forget not, that while you only hear and are delighted, you are still under nature's condemnation — and that the foundation is not laid, the mighty and essential change is not accomplished, the transition from death unto life is not undergone, the saving faith is not formed, nor the passage taken from darkness to the marvelous light of the gospel, till you are both hearers of the word and doers also.[2]

The *Astronomical Discourses* had an immediate impact. Huge crowds filled the church, and some businesses gave their employees half day holidays so that they could hear Chalmers. The sermons would also have a much wider impact through their subsequent publication. When Chalmers approached the Glasgow publisher John Smith (1784–1849) and asked him to consider publishing the *Discourses,* Smith hesitated, fearing that there was little money to be made in the publication of sermons, which had historically been the case. Smith suggested that Chalmers canvass his friends to ask for their financial backing for the project, but Chalmers refused on the grounds that it was demeaning to have to beg people for support. Smith, who was both a friend of Chalmers and a member of his congregation, eventually agreed to the venture and the risks involved, and he must have been glad that he did! Within ten weeks of publication, 6,000 copies of *The Discourses on the Christian Revelation, Viewed in Connection with Modern Astronomy* were sold and within a year 20,000 copies in nine editions had been purchased, making a tidy profit both for the author and the publisher.

One of Chalmers' gifts was self-promotion and he decided that if his new book was going to sell well, he would need to go on what would now be called an author tour. In the spring of 1817, he set out for London where he preached several sermons and became something of a sensation. While the book was already selling well, his personal appearances certainly helped to spread the word.

Encouraged by his London success, Chalmers returned to his Glasgow parish, more determined than ever to make an impact on the city. Increasingly he began to preach that the social impact of the gospel was being neglected. He told his congregation that the church tended to focus too much on the individual's relationship with Jesus Christ and hadn't spent enough time and energy showing people how they could have a real impact on the society as they lived out their faith. He sincerely believed that a revival of the evangelical faith within the Church of Scotland could make this possible. He also argued that all Protestants should be working together to create what he called "the godly commonwealth."

The concept of the godly commonwealth is critical to a proper understanding of Chalmers' thought and life. By it,

he meant that through the preaching of the gospel and the
inculcation of Christian principles a more moral, equitable
and just society would be created. For most of his life,
Chalmers would remain suspicious of government schemes
to improve the conditions faced by the poor. He believed
rather that the church could and should make a difference.
He did not believe that the church should simply become
an institution for the distribution of welfare, but rather that
the church, through Christian witness and in reliance on the
power of God, would make the rich care more for the poor
and the poor live lives that were shaped by the Christian
virtues of industry and responsibility.

Chalmers' desire to include other Protestants in his vision
for a renewed Scotland was not particularly controversial,
but his attitude toward the Roman Catholic Church was a
different matter. In December of 1817 he preached a sermon
before the Hibernian Society and took as his text Jesus' words
in Matthew 7:3–5:

> And why beholdest thou the mote that is in thy brother's
> eye, but considerest not the beam that is in thine own eye?
> … Thou hypocrite, first cast out the beam out of thine own
> eye; and then shalt thou see clearly to cast out the mote out
> of thy brother's eye.

In the sermon he called for greater tolerance and
understanding between Protestants and Catholics. He
claimed that much of the Protestant criticism of Catholicism
was based on prejudice and a misunderstanding that the
abuses of medieval Catholicism still had a grip on the
Catholic population. He went on to say that Protestants also
had their own failings and had no grounds to feel proud
of who they were. He argued that some of the prejudice

directed toward Roman Catholics was based as much on Protestant insecurities and a feeling of failure as it was on a clear understanding of Catholicism.

He also said that, if in a Protestant country,

> ... the majority of its inhabitants are utter strangers to the power [of the gospel]; and that an indifference to the matters of faith and eternity [exists, and if] the world engrosses every heart and the kingdom that is not of this world is virtually disowned and held in derision among the various classes and characters of society ... Call such a country reformed, as you may, [but] it is filled with the stronghold of antichrist from one end to another.[3]

While these harsh words have an element of truth in them, as they pointed to lack of concern for true Christianity, at the same time, they minimized the significant differences that existed between Roman Catholic dogma and reformed Protestant theology. Chalmers was right to call for deeper understanding between the various branches of Christendom and he was also right to call for increased toleration, but his views were overly romanticized and not entirely based in reality.

His Hibernian Society sermon created a sensation and, while some welcomed it, most evangelicals within the Church of Scotland believed that Chalmers had unwisely downplayed the real theological differences that existed. Chalmers was asked by his critics not to have the sermon published because they recognized that the power of the printed word would spread his ideas to a very wide audience. But he ignored their request. *The Discourse of Christian Charity Applied to the Case of Religious Differences* was published as an individual pamphlet, had a wide circulation and was subsequently included in his collected works.

Some of Chalmers' critics went so far as to question how any orthodox Church of Scotland minister could preach such a sermon. While this sermon may have given Chalmers a hearing in the wider world, he did find himself isolated for a time from those in the Church of Scotland who should have been his natural allies. This isolation affected him deeply, but it is unclear if he ever fully understood that it had largely been of his own making. His feelings of isolation were further intensified when his father died in July of 1818. He felt guilty that he hadn't treated his father better when he was a young man, and deeply regretted that his father's deafness and senility had prevented him from understanding that his son had become a sincere Christian and an evangelical minister.

Chalmers' successful venture into print with the *Astronomical Discourses* persuaded him that there was sufficient interest in his work, and a little money to be made, in the publication of his sermons. So, in 1819, he released through John Smith's publishing house, a collection entitled *Sermons Preached in the Tron Church Glasgow*. This collection was not a commercial success. Chalmers blamed the publisher for inadequate promotion of the book, but it is possible that the topic of the sermons, human depravity, didn't sound quite as interesting to potential readers as the subject of the *Astronomical Discourses* had. His blaming John Smith for the poor sales of this work would ultimately result in him switching publishers and it would mark the beginning of the very successful William Collins publishing house. Nonetheless these sermons give us an important insight into Chalmers' preaching, and more will be said about them in Chapter 10.

As Chalmers continued his work in the Tron parish he focused much of his energies on reaching out to the poorer people in the parish. As he did so, he experienced growing frustration that his ideal of what urban parish ministry should look like wasn't developing as he had hoped. What he really wanted was to recreate, in the urban context, what he had experienced in Kilmany. While this was naïve, Chalmers was passionate about the church meeting the needs of all those who needed help, both physical and spiritual.

He was especially frustrated by the way in which poor relief money was administered. While pew rents covered church expenses including ministerial stipends, separate collections were taken for the relief of the poor. These were controlled by the General Session, which was made up of ministers from each of the parishes. Money was then sent back to individual parishes based on the size of the poor population in the parish. If the needs outweighed the distributed funds then those cases were referred to the Town Hospital which was funded out of a local assessment.

Chalmers came to view this system as being overly complicated and began to campaign to keep all collections for the poor within the parish for the exclusive use of the parish. During 1818 and 1819 he increasingly advocated for the abolition of the system. In so doing, he clashed with other evangelicals in the Church of Scotland who believed that while the current system wasn't perfect, it was better than what Chalmers was advocating. One of Chalmers' failings was that he held his views with considerable tenacity and he wasn't always gracious when debating with others. So now, his views on poor relief and his personal manner, placed him at odds with those who should have been his natural allies in the Church of Scotland.

The Glasgow Town Council had been planning to create a new parish in the east end of Glasgow for some time. They had not planned on creating a new parish for Chalmers, but he seized upon the plans as a means of moving forward his vision for parish ministry in Scotland's cities. As he thought about implementing a fuller vision in a new parish, he was careful to ensure that wealthy pew holders at the Tron would be given the opportunity to move to the new parish if they chose. He also secured agreement that he could take some of the elders from the Tron to the new parish. This meant that he would be starting with a core congregation who could provide him with the manpower and the financial resources necessary to make the experiment work.

Chalmers ended his ministry at the Tron in July 1819, and the plan was for him to be installed as the minister of the new parish of St. John's in September. But the St. John's experiment almost didn't get off the ground. Chalmers had demanded assurances that he would be allowed to implement his own views on poor relief. However, the assurances were not forthcoming and, in fact, public opposition to his ideas was growing. As he waited to see what would happen, he left for Edinburgh to investigate the possibility of leaving the ministry entirely and instead, taking on the Chair of Natural Philosophy at the University of Edinburgh.

When it was announced that his name would be put forward for the chair at the university, there was intense negative reaction. He was accused by the press of abandoning all principles for the sake of personal advancement. Back in Glasgow, his supporters, who were looking forward to his ministry in the new parish felt betrayed and the elders, who were going to be serving on the Session of the new parish, threatened to resign.

Returning to Anstruther for a vacation, Chalmers finally recognized that his impulsive pursuit of the Edinburgh chair could result in him getting neither the pulpit at St. John's nor the academic appointment. He concluded that he needed to do some fence-mending and so reached out to one of his ministerial colleagues Andrew Thomson (1778–1831). Thomson was one of the leading evangelicals in the Church of Scotland and, although he had disagreed with Chalmers' views on Roman Catholicism and questioned whether or not his views on poor relief would work, he nevertheless wished Chalmers well in his new parish. As a result, he preached at the first service in St. John's parish church and formally introduced the new minister.

Chalmers had behaved impulsively as he explored the possibilities of moving to St. John's. He had upset many people in the Church of Scotland and on the Glasgow Town Council, but now he had the new parish that he desired. He could distribute poor relief in the way that he wanted, through the church, and it was now up to him to show whether or not this model of ministry would work.

Chapter 5
St. John's Parish
Glasgow 1819–1823

It is a little startling that St. John's was the first new parish church built in Glasgow in thirty years. Despite massive population growth, the town council had been reluctant to create new parishes because they were expensive to operate. Also, some argued that because there was little or no unrest in the city, no new churches were needed to help control the behaviour of the people. This is indeed a sad commentary on the motives behind church planting in the nineteenth century, but it was the reality.

Because of the reluctance to fund the building of new parishes at the end of the eighteenth century, the Church of Scotland had responded with the creation of Chapels of Ease. These chapels were not supported financially by town councils or patrons. They relied on the generosity of donors to support the minister. Unlike parish churches they were not set up along conventional Presbyterian lines. They did not have elders and they enjoyed the right of popularly electing their ministers. While the Chapels of Ease reached many with the gospel, they were not able to provide for the educational and temporal needs that many needed, and thus were not satisfactory substitutes for fully fledged parish churches.

While Chalmers' path to the pulpit of St. John's parish had not been straightforward, he nonetheless took on the challenges of the new work with his typical enthusiasm and vigour. As he did so he had a clear idea of what he hoped to achieve. He simply wanted to bring the message of the gospel and the lessons of Christianity into contact with the people of his parish. His first objective was to preach the gospel and through his preaching and teaching invite his hearers to repent of their sins and turn to Christ for salvation.

But there was more. What he had been able to do in Kilmany, partly because of its rural location and small population, he now hoped he would be able to do on a much grander scale. The four years that Chalmers spent as minister of this parish would do much to enhance his reputation. His preaching and writing increased his popularity, and it has been argued that during this period he revolutionized urban parish ministry in the Church of Scotland.

On 27 September 1819, just one day after his installation as the minister, Chalmers called the first meeting of the St. John's Committee of Education. He donated £100 of his own money and encouraged other people of means to show their commitment to parish education by making similar donations.[1] This was typical of the man. Once he had decided on a course of action, he would begin to work immediately to bring it about. Sufficient funds were raised so that by July of 1820, two schools in the same location were opened. The first school taught reading and English grammar while the second one taught writing, mathematics and book-keeping. School fees were charged but they were kept very low so as to make education affordable for as many people as possible. Chalmers took a very real interest in the running of the schools by visiting them regularly to encourage the teachers and to get to know the children better. Within a month of opening, the schools were overcrowded and the school masters were required to teach additional classes. By the time that he left Glasgow for St. Andrews in 1823, there were four parish schools that were providing education for four hundred and nineteen boys between the ages of six and fifteen.

One of Chalmers' achievements as minister of the Tron parish had been to reinvigorate the office of elder in the congregation. As we saw in the last chapter, he had recruited young men who had a vision for caring for the spiritual needs of the poor of the parish. Like the Tron parish, St. John's was divided into districts or proportions. In each of these Chalmers wanted to have an elder, a deacon and at least one Sunday School teacher. While he already had a good pool of elders to draw from, the situation with the deacons was different. While the Church of Scotland had long recognized this office, it had fallen into disuse particularly in the cities. But this was about to change.

Chalmers began to actively recruit men who could fill the ranks of the diaconate at St. John's. After a period of training, these men were ordained for the work. Each deacon was required to get to know the people who were in their district through regular visitation. They were not simply the instruments through whom charity was to be distributed; in fact, part of their job was to encourage self-reliance and family and community support for those in need. Chalmers was anxious to show his critics that with proper support from the church, the problem of pauperism could be reduced.

Chalmers expected his deacons to be proactive. They weren't to wait until problems presented themselves, instead, they were to be actively looking for opportunities to share their wisdom and provide support from church resources where that was necessary. The distribution of money from church offerings was an important part of their work, but it was not automatically given to all who asked for it. Rather, the deacons would first of all work with the needy to determine if there were others in their families who could help them, or to seek out ways for the needy to become more self-sufficient.

As part of their work, the deacons were required to meet together on a monthly basis to discuss common problems that they were facing and to strategize about how their work might be more effective. They were expected to become actively involved in dealing with the many social problems that existed in Glasgow. Their task included encouraging education and looking for ways to improve living conditions through the removal of health hazards and stressing the need for sobriety.

Chalmers' dream for St. John's was that lives would be changed through the preaching of the gospel, that his elders would provide pastoral care and oversight, and that the deacons would oversee the physical conditions in which the people were living. One of the side benefits of his plan for the parish was that it had a very positive impact on those who were doing the work of pastoral oversight, diaconal care and teaching. Chalmers was able to create a group of people who believed that they were making a difference in the world and their enthusiasm was infectious. To further encourage a positive spirit, Thomas and his wife Grace regularly hosted breakfasts and teas in their home for those who were involved in parish work. These meals provided encouragement for the workers, and also enabled Thomas to keep his finger on the pulse of the parish.

One of Chalmers' greatest gifts was that he was a very capable organizer. The pastoral work that was carried out showed his critics that a well-planned programme of evangelism, education and pastoral care could work. Thomas also led by example. While he was willing to delegate the bulk of the work to parish workers, he regularly made visits with his elders and deacons.

As Chalmers came to grips with the work of his parish he concluded that he needed an assistant to help him with the workload of preaching, teaching and visitation. When he heard of a young man by the name Edward Irving (1792–1834) and of his exceptional oratorical abilities, Chalmers went to hear him preach. Irving had graduated from the University of Edinburgh at the age of fourteen and had worked as a teacher for a time, while he set his sights on becoming a minister. He was eventually licensed to preach in June of 1815 but was unable to find a church which wanted to call him. Just as he was considering going on the mission field he was invited to take the assistantship of St. John's. There were four Sunday worship services in the parish: three in the church itself, and one in the school. William Hanna described how the work was divided:

> These four services were shared equally between Dr Chalmers and his assistant, the forenoon and evening service in the church on each alternate Sabbath devolving upon the one, the service in the school-house and the

afternoon service in the church devolving upon the other. Dr Chalmers commenced a series of lectures upon the Epistle to the Romans, and his assistant a series of lectures upon the Gospel of St. Luke. The same lecture which was delivered by each in the forenoon in the church was redelivered, but not on the same day, to the evening congregation, the series as preached in the forenoon being generally two or three lectures in advance of the series as delivered in the evening. It was particularly desired that the evening congregation should only consist of parishioners and those of the poorer classes whom the high seat rents charged upon the general or forenoon congregation served to exclude.[2]

Irving served for two years as the assistant minister at St. John's and in addition to his preaching, he spent a lot of time on parish visitation. During his brief tenure in the parish Chalmers developed a personal fondness for the young man, which he was to retain for the rest of his life.

Edward Irving's subsequent career is one of the tragic stories of nineteenth century Scottish church history. After leaving Glasgow, Irving served a church in London where he developed pronounced pre-millennial views on the second coming of Christ and taught these beliefs with eloquence and passion. He also began to teach ideas that would be precursors of the modern Pentecostal movement's stress on the supernatural gifts of the Spirit. Much more alarmingly, he developed and started teaching a heretical view of Christ's incarnation. He believed that Jesus' human nature was exactly like that of all other people, including the fact that it had "innate sinful propensities." He would go on to stress that Jesus was completely indwelt by the Holy Spirit from the moment of his conception, which enabled him to live a holy life. Not surprisingly, his critics pointed out that if Jesus had a sinful human nature, he too needed a saviour and thus was in no position to be offered as the perfect atonement for sin. Irving was deposed from the Church of Scotland ministry in 1833 and went on to found the Catholic Apostolic Church.

Chalmers has been criticized for his response to Irving's later life and particularly his descent into heresy. Some have even argued that Chalmers was completely unconcerned by Irving's unorthodox views, but there are passages in his diary and letters where he expressed concern about Irving's preaching and teaching. It is true that Chalmers took no part in any of the ecclesiastical trials which ended Irving's ministry in the Church of Scotland and in fact, Chalmers and his family retained a cordial relationship with Irving. But just as there were those who criticized Chalmers for not speaking out about Irving, there were also supporters of Irving who were distressed that Chalmers had not done more to help his former assistant. Chalmers' inaction, in this situation, does not reflect well on him. He cannot be accused of being a man who avoided conflict or difficult situations in his life, so his inaction did not stem from fear. But what does seem clear is that he allowed his feelings of personal affection for Irving to significantly cloud his judgment, and it would have been much better if he had spoken more clearly in this situation. It is a helpful reminder that friendships and feelings of personal loyalty, should not prevent Christians from speaking for truth or biblical orthodoxy. In this instance, Chalmers failed to do this.

In 1820 he published *The Application of Christianity to the Commercial and Ordinary Affairs of Life*. These eight sermons had formed part of the same mid-week series that had given the world the *Astronomical Discourses*. What is most striking in these sermons is that Chalmers is at pains to point out that true religion has implications far beyond the Christian's individual relationship with Christ and that true faith will impact all areas of life. In one of the sermons he said:

> ... the gospel of Jesus Christ does something more than hold out a refuge to the guilty.

> It takes all those who accept of its overtures under its supreme and exclusive direction. ... The grace which it reveals, is a grace that which not merely saves all men, but which teaches all men. He who is the proposed Saviour, also claims to be the (only) master of those who trust in him. His cognizance extends itself over the whole line of their history; and there is not an affection of their heart, or a deed of their visible conduct, over which he does not assert the right of an authority that is above all control, and that refuses all rivalship.[3]

Chalmers had taken the profits he had made from the hugely successful *Astronomical Discourses* and used them to set up his friend William Collins in the publishing business and it was under the Chalmers and Collins imprint that these sermons were published. Collins became the primary Scottish publisher of Chalmers' works, and the Collins publishing house would eventually become synonymous with quality publishing in Great Britain and around the world. It has been estimated that Chalmers' published works would make him as much as £14,000 in his lifetime.[4] (An approximate modern equivalent would be in the region of £1,400,000 or $1,800,000.) This was a significant amount of money and he used some of it to help fund his parish work and then later, to support the work of the Free Church after the Disruption in 1843.

His next publishing venture arose directly out of his work at St. John's. As he developed and implemented his ministry model, he released a series of quarterly papers which discussed his approach to the ministry. These were eventually gathered together and published in 1826 as *Christian and Civic Economy of Large Towns* and had a wide circulation. They received mixed reviews, with some questioning whether or not the essentially rural model of parish ministry could work in cities. Others welcomed and commended Chalmers' ideas.

By the autumn of 1821 Chalmers was beginning to feel tired because of all his labours in the parish. Although the four Sunday services and pastoral visitation were shared with his assistant, he also had to prepare for impromptu evangelistic meetings that took place in various locations throughout the parish during the week. It has been suggested that his more informal addresses at these meetings had a greater impact than his Sunday sermons did. Then in addition to all of this, there were all the meetings that he had to attend in order to keep all of the parish organizations running.

As he contemplated all of the work that needed to be done, Chalmers concluded that another congregation was needed to reduce his workload. He hoped that by planting another church in the parish that his workload would eventually be eased. The problem was that there were insufficient funds to create a fully-fledged parish and the Glasgow Town Council made it very clear to him that they were not going to erect a new parish. So, if a church was going to be built it would have to be done through private donations and be erected as a "Chapel of Ease."

In March of 1822 the St. John's session created a committee

to investigate the feasibility of establishing a chapel. Chalmers contributed £500 of his own money and persuaded others to contribute toward the project. He planned to use the donated funds to build the chapel and then pay back the contributions through a portion of the pew rents that the new congregation would generate. The fundraising work was difficult and it was only when someone from outside the parish contributed £1,000 that work on the building of the chapel could begin. Even when the initial funding was secured there were still other problems to deal with.

Many in the Glasgow presbytery weren't happy with the situation. There was bitterness because of the way in which Chalmers had gone about campaigning for his appointment to St. John's. Many were unconvinced that Chalmers' scheme for poor relief was working and they found willing supporters on the town council and in the press. There were increasing demands that door collections be handed over for the support of the Town Hospital rather than being used for poor relief in the area. At the Church of Scotland's General Assembly in May of 1822, Chalmers successfully argued his case that the new chapel should be allowed to keep the door collections for local poor relief, but it was a hard-fought victory. Chalmers was deeply hurt that most of the presbytery and the local government didn't share his vision. He took their objections very personally and it would be a very long time before he got over the hurt caused by this dispute.

While the chapel was being constructed, Chalmers was asked if he would consider accepting a call to a church in Edinburgh. He refused this offer but it is clear from his diary that he was feeling extremely tired from his parish work and he was beginning to wonder how long he could keep up with the workload. On 16 November 1822 he received a letter from Dr. Francis Nicoll (1770–1835) who was the Principal of the United Colleges of St. Leonard's and St. Salvador's at St. Andrews University. Nicoll told Chalmers that St. Andrews was seeking to fill the Chair of Moral Philosophy at the university and he asked if Chalmers would accept the chair if it were offered to him. Chalmers was somewhat surprised by this offer because Nicoll and the university were unsympathetic to Chalmers' evangelical theology, his interests and outlook. Nevertheless, he agreed to an interview, which took place in Edinburgh in January of 1823. Further letters were exchanged and later that month Chalmers agreed to the appointment.

On 18 January 1823 Chalmers was unanimously elected to the chair and two days later he called a meeting of St. John's elders, deacons and Sunday School teachers to inform them of his decision. At the meeting he read them his letter of resignation in which he told them that his decision was not an impulsive one. Further he indicated that he had had opportunities to leave St. John's earlier but had turned all of them down. So why was he leaving now? He told them he was resigning from the parish because his health would no longer allow him to keep up the pace of work that was required. He certainly had worked very hard and no one would ever accuse him of simply sitting in his study writing sermons. In fact, as we have seen, there was hardly an area of parish life that he had not involved himself in. He went on to say that with the opening of the Chapel of Ease and all the other programmes that were running so smoothly in the parish, he believed that the work of the ministry would carry on even if he were not there to oversee it. Another element in Chalmers' decision to move was his family. By now he and his wife had three daughters and Grace Chalmers was pregnant with their fourth. The prospect of moving from Glasgow to a rural location appealed to the whole family. Needless to say, most of his parishioners were very upset at losing their popular minister, but recognized that he would be doing good work for the wider church by teaching at the university, where he would come into contact with those training for the ministry.

Chalmers did not actually move to St. Andrews until November of 1823 so he was still the minister of St. John's when the new Chapel of Ease was opened in June of 1823. Although Chalmers was pleased that ministry in the chapel had finally begun, there was a significant outstanding financial debt. Because of this, the pew rents had to be set high so that the running costs of the chapel could be covered and a minister's stipend paid. While Chalmers had begun this project with the very best motives, the struggle to see the chapel completed had been an exhausting one. Then to his distress, the new chapel did not attract the number of people he had hoped for, and it would continue to struggle for stability for many years to come. Worse still from Chalmers' perspective was that the high pew rents meant that many people who he had hoped to reach with the gospel couldn't afford to attend the chapel.

Because the chapel was not a fully-fledged parish it was not allowed a local session of elders, so pastoral care and oversight had to be managed from St. John's. Additionally, as we have seen, one of the keys to Chalmers' successful parish ministry model at St. John's had been the momentum created by the training of new elders, deacons and teachers. This couldn't happen at the chapel and so the work was significantly hampered. When the chapel opened the decision was made to stop evening services at St. John's and move them to the chapel. This didn't encourage the development of a local congregation for the chapel. In retrospect, the chapel experiment was not a great success, and took away from Chalmers' undoubted achievements as the minister of St. John's.

There is much to admire in Chalmers' work during his tenure as the Minister of St. John's, however it must be conceded that his experiment in using funds raised from within the parish for poor relief was not a total success. Chalmers had incorrectly assumed that the rural parish ministry model could be fully implemented in a large city with a growing and mobile population. He had essentially underestimated the magnitude of the problems. Chalmers also staked a good deal of his own reputation on his work which meant that he found it very difficult to accept even constructive criticism. His writing and lecturing on his ministry model certainly raised his profile, but his greatest achievement at St. John's would ultimately prove to be his faithful preaching of the gospel. God blessed his ministry in such a way that many lives were changed and the evangelical party in the Church of Scotland was given a much higher profile and a wider hearing.

Chapter 6

St. Andrews University

1823–1828

Thomas Chalmers had been a student at St. Andrews in the last decade of the eighteenth century; he had taught there briefly, and before his conversion, had desperately wanted to obtain a permanent teaching post. The university was the oldest in Scotland, and the third oldest in Great Britain. Its roots went back to 1410 when a group of masters, mostly from France, initiated a school of higher studies in St. Andrews. By February 1411 the school had established itself sufficiently to receive a charter of incorporation and privileges from the Bishop of St. Andrews, Henry Wardlaw. Bishop Wardlaw soon began the process of applying for official university status. Only the Pope or the Emperor could confer this status and Wardlaw applied to Pope Benedict XIII (who was incarcerated in the Spanish fortress in Pensicola). On 28 August 1413 the Pope agreed to the petition but it would not be until February 1414 that the official documents arrived in St. Andrews to much celebration. The early history of the university was certainly eventful. In 1426, King James unsuccessfully tried to move the whole university to Perth. Then, in 1470, several masters and students were expelled for attacking the Dean with bows and arrows. Later in the sixteenth century the university banned beards, the carrying of weapons, gambling and football.

By the time of Chalmers' return to St. Andrews in 1823, the town had become something of a backwater. While the pace of the industrial revolution was having a significant impact on Scotland's biggest cities, the same could not be said of St. Andrews. In fact, during the first two decades of the nineteenth century the local economy had fallen on hard times. To be sure the town was rich in history, having seen John Knox preach there and Cardinal Beaton hung from the castle, but now only a feeling of faded grandeur remained.

The university had also seen better days. It had been decaying when Chalmers was a student, but now the situation was becoming very serious. Buildings were falling into disrepair and there were charges that money which had been set aside for improvements to the campus had in fact gone to augment the salaries of some of the faculty. As for the faculty, there were excellent teachers in some departments, but appointments were made based on family connections, friendships and political affiliation rather than academic excellence.

If the faculty were not particularly distinguished, neither was the student body. The resident student population was about two hundred and twenty, which was the smallest of Scotland's five universities. There were no entrance exams or requirements, and so most students simply transitioned from parish schools to the university at the average age of fourteen or fifteen. It should also be noted that the level of preparedness for university varied considerably among the student body.

The theological makeup of the St. Andrews faculty had not changed a great deal since Thomas Chalmers' student days. The moderate party in the Church of Scotland was still very much in control, and they could not have been too enthusiastic about adding an able and strong evangelical to their number. The appointment was in fact a pragmatic one. In voting for Chalmers, the faculty of the university was hoping that the popularity of the city preacher would attract desperately needed students. As we have already seen, Chalmers accepted the appointment partly for personal reasons, but also because he believed he would now have an opportunity to have an impact on the lives of young men who were preparing for ministry.

Chalmers moved by himself to St. Andrews in November of 1823, leaving his family behind in Glasgow until he could get himself established in his new location. He delivered his introductory lecture on Friday 14 November. He was pleased with how the lecture was received, but indicated in a letter to his wife that he wouldn't feel really settled until his family was able to join him, which they did in January of 1824.

His duties as Professor of Moral Philosophy were not arduous. His teaching responsibilities amounted to teaching one course per session. This was in sharp contrast to the exhausting pastoral duties he had just relinquished in Glasgow. If his teaching load wasn't heavy, he nonetheless made it clear that he was going to take the discipline in a new direction.

The teaching of moral philosophy at St. Andrews had long

followed in the tradition of the "Scottish common sense" school. This school of thought focussed on the study of the human mind so that it could be demonstrated that the mind had an internal moral regulator or "common sense" which reflected the divinely ordained moral dimension in the universe. The school taught that everyone had experiences that provided assurances of the existence of the self, the existence of real objects that could be seen and felt; and principles upon which sound morality and religious beliefs could be established. Perhaps not surprisingly Chalmers was about to take a very different approach to the subject.

On one level Chalmers accepted that individuals had a moral regulator, but this he called conscience. Where he most differed was in his understanding of what guided the conscience into making choices and decisions. Rather than seeing this as an innate human quality, he recognized that humanity needed to have their minds directed by God's revelation in Scripture. The thing that most shaped Chalmers' approach to his subject was his evangelical faith. In all that he taught he started with the assumption that salvation was necessary because of sin, and that salvation was only possible through faith in the crucified and risen Christ. He stressed that it was only as people were supernaturally freed from the power of sin and Satan by the work of the Holy Spirit that they were then able to live their lives in the community according to the positive principles taught in Scripture. Chalmers was also eager to show that it really mattered how people lived their lives. He further stressed that there were answers to society's problems which could be found in Scripture and that it was the duty of mankind to find these answers and to apply them. Rather than focussing in his teaching on epistemology, or the scope and nature of knowledge, Chalmers taught his students that what mattered most was the application of teachings of Scripture to the everyday problems that people faced in their lives and in society as a whole.

Chalmers was extremely popular with most of his students and was a charismatic teacher. His enthusiasm characterized his teaching. Unlike some of his colleagues who seemed to going through the motions as they taught, Chalmers delivered lively lectures. The same skills which he had used in the pulpit to draw large congregations in his Glasgow churches, he now used in teaching his students. Likewise, he used his gifts as a pastor to take a keen interest in their lives. He was known for very carefully grading student papers. Students came to recognize that when they submitted work to their professor he would take it seriously. His students were also encouraged to present seminars based on their papers. Exploration of new ideas was encouraged and perhaps most importantly, students were taught how to think for themselves. Although Chalmers was no twenty-first-century democrat in terms of his views on how society should be structured, he was insistent that all of his students should treat each other with respect and dignity, regardless of their background. For Chalmers all of his students were valuable and important.

During his second year at St. Andrews, he developed a new course on political economy. This gave him an opportunity to introduce his students to his political and economic views and to show them how he had sought to implement his ideas on poor relief during his time in Glasgow. This course was very popular, attracting thirty-five students the first time it was offered. He was seeking to show his students that his ideas were more than just theories; they had been tested and put into practice. Certainly, the students were given a somewhat one-sided and very positive view of Chalmers' great urban experiment, but they learned that ideas taught in the classroom needed to be worked out in the real world.

While Chalmers was extremely effective in the classroom, he also took it upon himself to actively mentor a small number of the young men. They were invited into his home on Sunday evenings for instruction and fellowship. While this group started very small, with no fanfare at all, word of it soon spread. So much so that "his large dining-room was [completely] crammed with students."[1]

Chalmers also took an interest in other areas of the university and the town. Not long after his arrival, he joined the St. Andrews Mission Society. Although this society had been in existence since 1812, it had ceased to be an active organization due to a lack of interest. Chalmers believed that if it could be revived it could enliven interest in foreign missions, and it might also play a key role in increasing the effectiveness of the evangelical party in the Church of Scotland. He presented to the Society a picture of the growth of Christian missions around the world, and pressed upon his hearers that it was the duty of the church to go into all the world to preach the gospel. He also expressed confidence in the power of the Holy Spirit to bless the faithful preaching of the gospel. Thus, he encouraged his hearers to think that there was hope for the world. His exciting presentations soon attracted such large audiences that the society had to move locations. The enthusiastic expansion of the town's missionary society soon spilled over into the university with one society starting up in the Divinity College and another in Chalmers' own moral philosophy class. These two university groups eventually merged to form the St. Andrews University

Missionary Society, with almost a third of the university's total student enrolment participating.

The St. Andrews Missionary Society met on a regular basis for prayer and study. In short order it became the most popular student organization at St. Andrews. The Society raised funds for foreign mission and created massive momentum that would eventually provide manpower for mission work. Alexander Duff, who would later be responsible for significant educational reform in India, was one student who was a member of the Missionary Society.[2] He gave full credit to the Society and the lecturing and preaching of Chalmers as the means that were used to interest him in missionary work.

Away from the university, Chalmers busied himself with other activities. He established a local Sabbath School in one of the poorest sections of the town. He invited the children to his home, where he told them Bible stories and undertook simple catechizing. In doing this, Chalmers was demonstrating his genuine passion for the spread of the gospel to those who might never have been inside a church. While he was personally engaged in this work, he also actively encouraged some of the young men in his classes to become involved as teachers in Sabbath Schools in other parishes of the Church of Scotland. When some of them met resistance, he suggested that they might find greater acceptances if they offered their services to some of the dissenting congregations in the area that were not part of the Church of Scotland but who did have an evangelical outlook.

As this student work gained momentum, Chalmers was presented with a proposal to open a summer school that would give free instruction in economics, history, mathematics and philosophy. While he truly appreciated the desire that lay behind this proposal, he was concerned that the students' enthusiasm might be greater than their abilities to make it work, and so he reluctantly suggested that this was not a good idea.

All of this activity in St. Andrews shows that while Chalmers may have felt the need to leave active parish ministry, he had not escaped into an ivory tower. His lectures were inspiring and instructing a new generation of students and he was, along with his students, putting into practice one of his basic principles that the gospel must be lived out. For Chalmers, faith that remained in the head but did not warm the heart and change lives, was not genuine.

While Chalmers' classroom lectures and relationships with students were a success the same cannot be said for his interactions with the university's faculty and administration or with some in the Church of Scotland. One area of conflict was over the eligibility of Church of Scotland ministers to hold appointments both at the university and also in a parish. In 1824 Francis Nicoll, who was both the Principal of the United Colleges and minister of the college chapel, requested that an assistant minister for the chapel be appointed. Nicoll had come to realize that he couldn't do both of his jobs well without help. He proposed that James Hunter (1772–1845), the university's Professor of Logic and Rhetoric, be given the position. Hunter was well liked and the proposal seemed uncontroversial but Chalmers reacted angrily. He argued strenuously that Hunter should not be appointed the assistant at the chapel unless he was going to resign his academic appointment. He went further and turned on Nicoll, who had been instrumental in his own appointment, and suggested that if he needed help doing two jobs then he should resign as minister of the chapel and devote himself to his academic work.

Nicoll, who had viewed Chalmers as a friend, made a personal appeal to him, but his request went unheeded. Chalmers instead took his complaints to the local presbytery and at the same time began to organize opposition to the appointment. As tensions built, both moderates and evangelicals appealed to Chalmers to behave appropriately, as he was bringing both the church and the university into disrepute. But he pressed on. Eventually Nicoll succumbed to pressure and resigned as the minister of the chapel and Hunter was appointed in his place, while still keeping his academic chair. But this did not end the unpleasantness. Some evangelical students broke university regulations by refusing to attend services in the chapel that were led by Hunter and demanded to be allowed to go to other churches. While Chalmers claimed he hadn't put the students up to this, he nevertheless was quietly supportive of them. Eventually tensions eased but the damage had been done.

Chalmers' behaviour in this incident appears to have been motivated by his genuine belief that a minister shouldn't hold more than one appointment, and also his suspicion that too many academics weren't hard working enough. But even if he was acting out of principle, he did not conduct himself well. He had drawn students into a dispute that was not their concern, and he had paid little attention to his personal relationships with his colleagues on the faculty. How he thought he could remain as an effective member of the university community when he had lost a lot of good will, is something he doesn't seem to have thought about very much.

Chalmers' relationship with the university faculty and

administration deteriorated further when he decided to take up the question of how funds were being spent by the university. It had been the practice since 1784 to pay the faculty an annual dividend to supplement what were admittedly small stipends. Shortly after his arrival at the university, Chalmers came to the principled conclusion that he and the other faculty were not entitled to this money and so he announced he would not take the money for himself, and that he was considering referring the whole matter to the civil courts for investigation. His concern was that funds which should have gone for university improvements were instead going into the pockets of the professors.

Eventually the government in London, faced with unrest at St. Andrews and other Scottish universities, decided to set up a Royal Commission to investigate the whole matter. Chalmers was called as a witness in the summer of 1827. He gave lengthy evidence in which he spoke out against plural appointments, the special dividend paid to faculty, and he further called for reform of the curriculum to bring it more up to date. Before the Commission brought in their final report they indicated to Chalmers that the payment of the dividend to the faculty was probably legal. So, on the basis of this he accepted his share of it in 1829. When the final report was delivered in 1831, it was decreed that the dividend should not have been paid and plural appointments were condemned. While the Commission's report provided some vindication for Chalmers' original concerns, he appeared totally inconsistent for having accepted the 1829 dividend.

Chalmers' outspoken criticisms of the administration of the university alienated him further from his colleagues, and so he began to wonder if he should be looking for another position. Through most of 1827 Chalmers seriously considered an offer to move to the University of London to take the Chair of Moral Philosophy there, but then in 1828 he heard that the Edinburgh Town Council had elected him to the prestigious Chair of Theology at the University of Edinburgh. During his years at St. Andrews, Chalmers had remained in contact with the people of Edinburgh and Glasgow through regular preaching, and there is little doubt that his oratorical skills contributed as much to his new appointment as they had to the one at St. Andrews. With the sense that God was calling him to a new and more important field of labour, he accepted the appointment.

Chalmers' time in St. Andrews was something of a mixed blessing for him. There was personal happiness for him as two of his daughters were born there, but he also lost his much-loved mother and sister. In summarizing this period of his life, his biographer William Hanna wrote:

> He was known to be a man of prayer; he was acknowledged to be a man of active benevolence. He was observed to be going about from house to house, exhorting adults on the concerns of their salvation, and devoting his energies to the humble task of gathering around him a Sabbath School. He was seen to be the sole reviver of an all but defunct missionary society.[3]

As a result of his character, example and teaching, he had a major impact on the lives of a number of young people who would subsequently go on to do much good for the church throughout the world. However, as has been noted, he increasingly found himself in the middle of controversy. It was a period when he lost friends, made unnecessary foes, and his inability to get along with people he did not agree with, became much more pronounced.

Chapter 7
The Scottish Church
Crisis 1828–1842

The period from 1828–1842 was among the busiest of Chalmers' life. During this period, he occupied the Chair of Divinity at the University of Edinburgh, which meant he was teaching and tutoring students. Just as importantly, he became increasingly involved in the ecclesiastical politics of the Church of Scotland that led to the Disruption of May 1843, and the creation of the Free Church of Scotland.

Chalmers was inaugurated as the Professor of Divinity at the University of Edinburgh on 6 November 1828 and his inaugural lecture took place on the following Monday. William Hanna, described the scene in these terms:

The morning of that day was singularly unpropitious, showers of snow and hail sweeping through College courts; yet from so early an hour as nine, those who had secured that privilege were passing by a private entrance into the classroom, while so great a crowd besieged the outer door, that a string of police found it difficult to restrain the tumult.[1]

During the winter of 1828–29, Chalmers was extremely busy. His lectures at the university were very well received. He became so occupied with work that he asked his household servants to protect him from intruders who merely wanted to have a social visit with him.

In 1829, one of the most controversial political debates of the early nineteenth century began when it was announced that the government was going to pursue a policy of Roman Catholic emancipation. This was a major change for Britain. In 1661 Parliament had passed a series of laws which were largely designed to protect the realm from the influence of Roman Catholicism. These pieces of legislation prevented all those who were not members of the established church, and specifically Roman Catholics, from sitting in Parliament or holding public office. Under the terms of the proposed emancipation legislation, members of the Roman Church and Protestant non-conformists, would have the same political rights and freedoms as citizens who belonged to the established church. This decision received a mixed response. Many evangelicals opposed the proposals, but Chalmers was quick to agree with the new policy.

As we have already noted, when he was at the Tron Church, he had called for greater toleration and understanding between Protestants and Catholics, and he had renewed this call in a sermon delivered at the opening of Edward Irving's church in London on 11 May 1827. In this sermon he reminded his hearers that one of the great benefits of the work of the reformers such as Martin Luther and John Knox was that they had,

> ... cleared away a most grievous obstruction which had stood for ages and intercepted from mankind the light of the book of revelation. This they did, by asserting, in behalf of God, the paramount authority of his Scriptures over the belief and consciences of men; and asserting in behalf of man his right of private judgement ... This right of private judgement, you will observe is a right maintained not against the authority of God, but against the authority of men, who either added to the oracles of God, or who have assumed to themselves the office of being infallible and ultimate interpreters of his word.[2]

Having cited this as one of the great benefits of the Reformation, he then went on to criticize some Protestants for unnecessarily infringing on the right of private judgement by imposing on Roman Catholics and non-conformist Protestants strictures that the Scriptures did not require.

Then on 1 April 1829, he gave another address in Edinburgh where he brought his argument to its conclusion. He stated that there was no need, or any theological justification, for preventing Catholics from taking part in the political and public life of the country. He argued that the suppression of Catholicism by legal means was wrong. He contended that reason, Scripture and prayer were the weapons that God had given to the church for the propagation of the gospel. Instead of maintaining laws that suppressed others, the Protestant church should rely on the power of the Holy Spirit to advance the cause of Christ. He concluded with: "Our single defence against one and all is to out preach, out pray and outlive them ... Our sentiment is that Protestantism can uphold itself."[3]

One of the results of Catholic emancipation and the subsequent Reform Act of 1832, which expanded the electoral franchise, was the weakening of the old assumption that the government had a duty to support the established church. While Chalmers did not believe that Catholics and non-conformists should be persecuted for their views, he still held firmly to the belief that it was the duty of the State to support the work of the established church, the Church of Scotland.

Increasingly, Chalmers' pastoral and teaching experience, along with his writings, meant that his profile as an important leader and thinker grew. In 1830, he gave evidence before a Select Committee of the House of Commons on the issue of poor relief in Ireland. In his evidence, he argued that the government should be providing support to the established churches and then allowing them to administer poor relief through the parish system. Chalmers also told the committee that the parish system as he had seen it working in Kilmany and as he had tried to implement it in Glasgow was the best way forward. Chalmers firmly believed that those who were in need must first have their character reformed through the teaching of the church and the embracing of Christian values, and only then would they benefit from poor relief. He was also concerned with a broader issue, that of the secularization of society. As he saw the impact of the industrial revolution and rapid population growth, he was becoming increasingly alarmed that the old values were being lost. It was therefore essential to put the church at the heart of the poor relief system, so that people could be helped spiritually as well as physically. The committee chose to ignore most of his advice and, in fact, didn't reach any firm conclusions at all, other than to tell Parliament the issue needed further study!

Undeterred by his failure to persuade Parliament, Chalmers chose to expand his ideas and publish them. These appeared in 1832 in a book entitled *On Political Economy, in Connexion with the Moral State and Moral Prospects of Society.* The book received mixed reviews, with some welcoming Chalmers' thesis that the church should be the source of poor relief, while others dismissed it, arguing that it was only the national government which could adequately execute this task. Chalmers' belief that governmental poor relief programmes would only serve to further secularize the society may have been correct, but the mood of the day was not in his favour.

This book was just the latest example of Chalmers' prodigious literary output. By the time of his death in 1847, Chalmers' publications would reach an astounding twenty-five volumes with nine more volumes published after his death. A good deal of the credit for this massive productivity must be given to Grace Chalmers, Thomas's wife. She handled all of the publishing arrangements with his publisher, William Collins, and answered most of his correspondence. This, in addition to all of the duties of a pastor and professor's wife and mother of six daughters, indicates what a remarkable woman she was.

On 9 February 1831, the Reverend Andrew Thompson (who had preached the first sermon at St. John's Parish Church in Glasgow) died suddenly of a heart attack. At the time of his death, he was the minister of St. George's parish church in Edinburgh, and was considered by many as the leader of the evangelical wing in the Church of Scotland. Although Chalmers and Thompson had much in common, they did not always see eye to eye. Thompson never agreed with Chalmers' idea that poor relief should be exclusively distributed through the parish system and, in fact, had been a supporter of government plans for the strengthening of the poor laws. Despite these differences, Chalmers preached at his funeral, choosing as his text the words from Hebrews 11:4:

"He being dead yet speaketh." In the sermon he encouraged Thompson's congregation to remember their minister for who he was, what he had taught and most of all for his evangelical faith, which Chalmers said, was the belief "by which alone the righteousness of the life and practice was upholden. He was truly a preacher of faith … [and] charity of that love in the heart which prompts to all the services of humanity."[4]

Chalmers assumed Thompson's mantle as the leader of the evangelicals, which impacted the rest of his life and ministry. The first public recognition of his increased prominence was his election as the moderator of the General Assembly of the Church of Scotland in 1832. He carried out his duties with distinction. He was seen to referee debates with fairness and won the approval of both the moderate and evangelical parties in the Assembly.

During 1833, Chalmers' profile in Edinburgh and throughout the Scottish church continued to grow. He found himself in the middle of a highly contentious debate about how the clergy in Edinburgh should be paid. The town council wanted to abolish the Annuity Tax, the revenues from which had paid clergy stipends. What particularly angered Chalmers was the council's proposal that the number of clergymen in Edinburgh should be reduced and that the rest of the clergy should have their stipends cut. Debate raged at both the town council and in the presbytery about the best way forward. Another element of the debate was that the church was increasingly having to contend with the rising tide of voluntarism, the belief that the church should be supported only by those who attended and not from government revenues. If the council's proposals were approved, it would be a direct threat to the privileged position of the Church of Scotland. Chalmers passionately believed that it was the established church that could best bring about the vision of the godly commonwealth. His dream could only be realized if the church would have enough money so that it would be less dependent on pew rents for operating capital. He believed that if the church were financially independent, the poor would be able to come to church on the same basis as the wealthy and stability in society would be maintained through Christian teaching and principles.

In April 1833, the presbytery of Edinburgh appointed Chalmers to its committee for the preservation of presbytery's endowments and income. His appointment was due in part to his rising prominence, but it also was because his stipend came to him as a result of his university appointment. As a result, he was perceived as not being directly impacted by the strenuous debate that was taking place.

In January 1834, the town council did in fact eliminate the Annuity Tax and reduced the number of clergy serving Church of Scotland congregations in Edinburgh. Chalmers was very angry with this decision. At a meeting of the Edinburgh presbytery on 23 January 1834, he raised the alarm that the mission of the church was under attack from the Voluntary Movement and the town council. He passionately argued that unless the church continued to have proper funding from the government, it would never be able to care for the needs of those who needed the gospel the most. The presbytery was energized by his speech and enthusiastically adopted his committee's report, even though the battle over the tax was lost.

Not only did Chalmers and the church not achieve their goals, but the strain of recent events took an immediate toll on his health. On his way home from the presbytery meeting, he suffered what was, in all probability, a stroke. He was paralyzed on his right side, although he was still able to communicate clearly. There was real concern as to whether or not he would completely recover. Chalmers confided in letters and in his diary his fears that he might lose his mental faculties and might not regain his physical strength. However, he did recover sufficiently that he was able to return to his teaching duties at the University of Edinburgh. Towards the summer he suffered a relapse with what he described as "considerable and constant noise" in his head. When this occurred, his doctor insisted that he cease all study and spend the summer having a complete rest. Chalmers' restless personality made it difficult for him to relax but he had little choice. His cousin Charles Cowan provided Thomas, his wife and two of his daughters with comfortable accommodation for the summer which allowed for a period of recuperation.

As we saw earlier, when discussing Chalmers' ministry in Glasgow, the Church of Scotland had been almost entirely unsuccessful in the first years of the nineteenth century in gaining government grants for the establishment of new parishes. Many recognized that there was a need but no one wanted to pay for it. As a result, the Church of Scotland began to look for other solutions, and at the 1834 General Assembly plans were put in place in an attempt to move the work of the church forward.

Chalmers was unable to be actively involved in the Assembly because of his health, but this did not stop him from being a very interested observer or expressing his opinions. Despite his poor health and the lack of certainty about his recovery, the Assembly asked Chalmers to chair a new committee on church extension, which was known as the Church Accommodations Committee. The aims of this committee were twofold: first, to lobby the government for more funds, and secondly, to seek private donations if money from the government was not forthcoming. As Chalmers began to recover during the summer months, he set the work of the committee in motion and, as he was able, took an enthusiastic part in its work. Chalmers was very clear on the committee's goal: to open as many Church of Scotland parishes as were needed to serve the needs of the population so that everyone who wanted to go to church could. It was not too long before what had begun as the work of a church became a movement.

This period coincided with a revival in evangelical religion in Scotland. As Chalmers began his work for this committee, the seed he was sowing fell on hungry and fertile ground. He took every speaking engagement that he could to explain his vision; in addition, he had a captive and motivated audience in his classroom at the University of Edinburgh. For many of his divinity students, the only way that they could ever hope to find a vacant pulpit would be if there was significant expansion within the Church of Scotland. So, Chalmers encouraged his students to take his message outside the university classroom to the people of Scotland. The message was a simple one. The Great Commission given by Jesus to his disciples needed to be carried out, and society's good demanded that people should be able to hear the gospel and receive Christian education and discipleship from a local congregation.

Also, at the 1834 General Assembly, the Veto Act was passed. The purpose of this act was to restrict the power of patronage by giving to male heads of families the right to veto the parish patron's appointment of their local minister. Chalmers enthusiastically supported this piece of legislation, and argued for it on the basis that the church could trust the common sense of its members to make proper appointments. To modern ears, this hardly seems a noteworthy event, but it was very controversial at the time. The first test of the Veto Act occurred in 1834 in the parish of Auchterarder, Perthshire, where out of a total of three hundred and thirty-six heads of families, only two of them were prepared to sign a call to the laird's preferred candidate, Robert Young. When the call was not then acted upon by the presbytery, Young sued, thus beginning a long legal wrangle.

The same General Assembly also passed the Chapels Act. This act gave official recognition to Chapels of Ease granting them similar status as parish churches.[5] This had the immediate effect of swelling the ranks of the evangelical party in the Church of Scotland. With the Veto Act and the Chapels Act in place, the Church of Scotland began an aggressive and impressive church extension programme, which would see the building of many churches and schools throughout Scotland. Rather than asking for full government financial support for this expansion programme, the church decided to fund this effort largely through private contributions. They only looked to the government to provide a partial endowment in those areas where poverty was so great that parish residents could not afford to pay the stipends of the local school master and minister. Chalmers' visionary leadership of the Church Accommodations Committee turned it into a movement that produced significant funds for the establishment of new churches.

Chalmers' increasing reputation was recognized by an important honour he received in 1834. He was surprised to be elected as a corresponding member of The Royal Institute of France. He felt deeply honoured to receive this recognition for his academic work. However, it would not be until 1838 that he was able to visit France to accept this award. He travelled with Charles Cowan, who acted as his translator. In Paris he was greeted with real warmth as he preached at the Chapelle Taitbout and also gave a scholarly paper to the Institute. A second honour was given to him in 1835 when the University of Oxford awarded him a Doctor of Laws degree. In doing so, the university singled out his academic work, along with his pioneering work in parish ministry and his leadership in the Church of Scotland. While Chalmers cannot be faulted for his energy and vision in leading the cause of church extension, he was not as successful in persuading those who disagreed with him to join his cause.

Chalmers was a very complex character. He could be very stubborn and possessed a formidable temper, which he displayed all too often. His pen, which he had used so successfully to promote the gospel and social change, could sometimes be turned on his foes. In 1834, for example, as the Edinburgh Town Council continued their campaign to reduce the number of ministers, he published a fiery pamphlet entitled, *On the Evils which the Established Church in Edinburgh Has Already Suffered, and Suffers Still, in Virtue of the Seat-Letting Being in the Hands of the Magistrates.* Pamphlets like this one only hardened people's positions rather than bringing about resolution. It was typical of Chalmers' approach when he was challenged or thwarted.

Chalmers' relationship to the British Government's Royal Commission on Religious Instruction in Scotland presents another example of the complexity of his character. The Commission was given a broad remit to investigate the need for more churches that would receive government support or endowment. While Chalmers was concerned about the composition of the Royal Commission he nonetheless counselled patience. He believed that the Commission would have enough information to make the correct decision and recommend greater support for the Church Extension Movement in Scotland. However, when an Edinburgh minister, Robert Lee, gave evidence that Chalmers' parish model didn't really work in the cities, Chalmers reacted with fury.

His outburst was prompted by the fact that Lee had been nominated as the moderator of the 1836 General Assembly. Chalmers had initially nominated Lee, but he quickly changed his mind when Lee's evidence contradicted his views. Chalmers was successful in blocking the appointment in 1836, but when the nomination was reissued the following year his opposition became even more pointed. In January of 1837 he published another pamphlet called *A Conference with Certain Ministers of the Church of Scotland, on the Subject of the Moderatorship of the Next General Assembly.* Chalmers named Lee in the pamphlet and engaged in a bitter personal attack against his ministerial colleague. Many of his friends believed he had gone too far, and for a time his image was tarnished by his impulsive behaviour. It is unfortunate that his quick temper sometimes got the better of him. While his explosions were often of a public nature, they do not present a fully rounded picture of the man. He was much loved by his family and friends and wrote witty and warm letters to his wife and daughters when he was away from them.

Chalmers was a prodigious letter writer, corresponding with people on both sides of the Atlantic. One of his correspondents was John Strachan, the Anglican Bishop of Toronto. While Strachan and Chalmers differed on many theological issues, they maintained a lively correspondence over many years. Strachan even invited Chalmers to visit Toronto in 1841. Chalmers declined on the grounds of poor health and the demands on his time, but nonetheless thanked him for his "kind and affectionate invitation."[6]

Between 1834 and 1843, the church scene in Scotland became increasingly complex as tensions increased both within the Church of Scotland and among the church, the courts and the British government. While Chalmers was not directly involved in all of these situations, it is important that we understand what was going on in the wider scene.

Within the church, evangelicals were continuing to call for the people to have the freedom to call their own ministers. There were several cases that brought this issue to the forefront of the public's mind. The most notable instance took place in the Parish of Marnoch when John Edwards was presented as the next minister. While he had the support of the patron, the congregation didn't want him to be their minister. The local innkeeper was the only member of the parish to sign the call which created a major problem for the presbytery whose job it was to install the new minister. The presbytery asked the Commission of Assembly (who were tasked with making decisions between General Assemblies) what they should do. They were instructed to reject the nomination, which they did. The patron accepted this decision, but Mr. Edwards did not, and he subsequently took the presbytery to court. The presbytery responded by saying that they would await the result of the court action before making a final decision. In the end, the civil Court of Session instructed the presbytery of Strathbogie to proceed with Edwards' installation but the church's Commission of Assembly told them not to. Faced with the difficult decision of having to choose between obeying the state or the church, the presbytery met and agreed by a vote of seven to four to obey the civil court and sustain Edwards' ordination. The

'Strathbogie Seven' as they were called, were subsequently deposed for disobeying the church, and the minority were called upon to announce the sentence of deposition. Eventually Edwards was admitted as minister of the parish, while the seven suspended ministers constituted themselves as the presbytery and sought court protection to keep those who opposed them out of the area. This case had much wider implications than in the particular parish involved, because it brought into sharp relief divisions within the church over how ministerial calls should be handled.

On the political front, the British government announced that they would not support the work of the church in the poorer areas where the partial endowments had been sought. This was a blow to the church that had hoped to at least get some funding for the creation of much needed parishes. Then the Court of Session in Scotland decided that the church's Veto Act was illegal, since it infringed on the rights of parish patrons to choose the minister. These decisions effectively killed the momentum that had been created by the Church Extension Movement. Undoubtedly, there had been real progress. From the time that the campaign started until Chalmers resigned from the committee in 1841, over £300,000 was raised and two hundred and twenty-two new churches were built. To even the most critical or cynical of observers, the scheme was a massive success.

By 1842 the situation was reaching a breaking point. Frustration was growing because the state, through the courts, was inserting itself into issues that were none of its business. Over the next eighteen months events were set in motion which would change the face of the church in Scotland. And Thomas Chalmers stood at the centre of these events.

• Tanfield Hall, Canonmills.—First General Assembly, 1843 •

Chapter 8
The Disruption 1842–1843

As if the divisions between the moderates, who were more or less happy with the status quo, and the evangelicals, who wanted change, were not enough, it became increasingly apparent during 1842, that the evangelicals were not in total agreement on the way forward for the church. As we have seen, Chalmers was firmly opposed to those who believed that patrons should be left alone to choose parish ministers, however, he also wanted to maintain government financing for an established church. While the evangelicals were all agreed that congregations should have a direct say in the appointment of their ministers and wanted the church to be spiritually independent, not everyone was as convinced that an established church was a good idea.

Robert Candlish (1806–1873), the minister of St. George's Church in Edinburgh, was just one influential figure who came to believe that a connection with the state might be detrimental for the church.[1] At a meeting of the Edinburgh presbytery in January 1842, he stated that the only way to end the uncertainties and disputes currently raging would be for the church to recognize that patronage and connection to the state might need to end. He went on to argue that the really important thing was that the church should never compromise on the principle of spiritual independence.

> I prefer the downfall of the Establishment infinitely rather than any compromise of principle. Of the two things — the Church existing as a Voluntary Church, or existing as a Church Establishment with even an apparent sacrifice of honour or of principle — I am convinced that her existence as a Voluntary Church is far more likely to promote the glory of God and to win souls to Christ.[2]

In telling the story of the birth of the Free Church it is easy to focus on the work of clergy like Chalmers and Candlish, but it is important to note here that it would be as much a creation of the laity. Hugh Miller (1802–1856) was an important figure at this time. He was a stone mason by profession, an accomplished amateur geologist and a journalist. As the dispute over the spiritual independence of the church continued, he wrote strenuously in support of the evangelical cause. He expressed his opinions so strongly that he would eventually be encouraged to launch his own newspaper, *The Witness*. Starting with only six hundred subscribers, the paper would eventually rival *The Scotsman* as a shaper of public opinion. It is important to note here that the debates taking place in presbytery meetings were becoming much more public. Through Miller's colourful journalism, popular support for the spiritual independence of the church was increasing.

Another important figure was Chalmers' cousin Charles Cowan (1801–1889) who was a successful businessman, philanthropist, politician and churchman. A. Donald

MacLeod, Cowan's biographer, states that "Cowan would be in thrall to Chalmers" all his life and that "there is evidence to suggest … Chalmers regarded him almost as the son he never had." Cowan was devoted to Chalmers' vision for a church that would spread the good news and care for the people of Scotland. Their family relationship, combined with Cowan's business acumen, meant that he was ideally suited to help with planning for the financial viability of the new church.[3]

In March 1842, yet another group in the church emerged. The "middle party" claimed that they didn't want the state intruding in the affairs of the church, but advocated further negotiations with the government in hopes that compromises could be reached. They called for calm since they believed that Chalmers and other leading evangelicals were being far too strident. This group attracted a number of leading moderate evangelicals to their cause and their ranks eventually comprised about 40 ministers, some from quite prominent churches. Chalmers wasn't impressed by their argument for moderation, and neither were most of his followers. In the pages of *The Witness*, Hugh Miller accused these men of wanting to compromise only so that they could hang onto their stipends and their manses. He charged them with selling out the cause, and dubbed them "the forty thieves." Despite Miller's attacks, there were suggestions that the government might hear the pleas from the middle party and agree to recognize the stipulations of the Veto Act as long as the church wouldn't continue to be so outspoken on the issue of spiritual independence. However, events were reaching the point of no return.

The future direction of the Church of Scotland came into much sharper focus during the General Assembly which took place in Edinburgh in May 1842. The tone for the Assembly was set at the very beginning when there was a wrangle over which representatives from the presbytery of Strathbogie should be seated. Rival groups from the presbytery appeared, each claiming the right to take part. On the one side were representatives of those who had obeyed the civil courts and installed John Edwards as the minister of the Parish of Marnoch, even though this was against the majority opinion of the parish. On the other side was a delegation representing those who had deposed the so-called "Strathbogie Seven" for disobeying the church.

Some argued that the representatives of those who had obeyed the Commission of Assembly, and had deposed the "Strathbogie Seven," should be allowed to take their seats and take part in the Assembly. The moderate minority of the church argued that neither should be seated because the church was so divided on the issue. Further, there were still appeals to be heard on the merits of the original case. Chalmers argued that the Assembly had no choice but to seat those who had been obedient to the church. He also stated that if the moderates didn't like this, they should either secede from the church or themselves face disciplinary action. The Assembly backed Chalmers, but this wasn't the end of the story. The Court of Session ruled that the Assembly was acting illegally and forbade the members of the Strathbogie presbytery from participating. In response, the Assembly ignored the ruling of the court, claiming that their decision was just another example of unjust civil interference in the affairs of the church. If anyone had thought that this Assembly might bring about a peaceful resolution to the crisis, it was pretty clear now that this was not going to be the case.

The General Assembly of 1842 has come to be associated

with two pieces of ecclesiastical legislation. First, a resolution was passed which called on the government to totally abolish patronage. This motion was proposed by William Cunningham (1805–1861) who would go on to become one of the most influential Scottish theologians of the nineteenth century. Chalmers was unenthusiastic about this measure because he still held out hope that the government might recognize the spiritual independence of the church while maintaining some form of financial support for the church. However, he was concerned that the evangelical wing of the Church of Scotland was beginning to fragment, so against his better judgement, he supported this motion.

On Tuesday, May 24, Chalmers moved the adoption of the other important piece of legislation "The Claim, Declaration and Protest, Anent the Encroachments of the Court of Session." It was the clearest possible statement that the Church of Scotland should be free from all interference on spiritual matters, such as the selection of ministers and issues of church discipline. After reciting the history of church and state relations, the document concluded by recognizing:

> ... the absolute jurisdiction of the Civil Courts in relation to all matters whatsoever of a civil nature, and especially in relation to all the temporalities conferred by the State upon the Church, and the civil consequences attached by law to the decisions, in matters spiritual, of the Church Courts,— DO, in name and on behalf of this Church, and of the nation and people of Scotland, and under the sanction of the several statutes, and the Treaty of Union herein before recited, CLAIM, as of RIGHT, that she shall freely possess and enjoy her liberties, government, discipline, rights, and privileges, according to law, especially for the defence of the spiritual liberties of her people, and that she shall be

protected therein from the foresaid unconstitutional and
illegal encroachments of the said Court of Session, and her
people secured in their Christian and constitutional rights
and liberties.

In his speech supporting this legislation, Chalmers made
the point that the church would never surrender its historic
rights, but if the British (and here he actually used the word
English) government continued on the present course, there
would be no option but for evangelicals within the church
to give up state support. The Claim of Right, as the act came
to be known, easily passed the General Assembly and was
dispatched to London. The Conservative government in
London responded almost immediately by admitting that
they couldn't find an immediate solution to the problem and
left it to the civil courts to determine the rights and wrongs of
the various cases in dispute.

Thomas Chalmers and his family headed for Ireland after
the Assembly for a period of rest, but he still kept a careful
eye on the fast-developing events. In August, the House of
Lords in London took a decision, which effectively quashed
any hopes for the spiritual independence of the church. In
effect, they said that any minister or elder who believed in
the arguments presented in the Claim of Right no longer
belonged in the church.

Returning from Ireland, Chalmers and his colleagues began
to make plans for what would not be another minor secession
from the church but which had the potential to reshape the
entire church landscape. As they began planning the next
steps, it was not entirely clear how many ministers, elders
and their congregations would be prepared to sacrifice their
livelihoods, church buildings and manses for the sake of

principle. There were probably those in the government in London, serving on courts in Scotland and within the church, who hoped that this was all a bluff, and that Chalmers and the other leaders would never be able to keep their supporters with them. It is at this point that many people underestimated just how effective a leader Chalmers was.

Chalmers returned to Scotland at the beginning of September 1842. Over the course of the autumn, he began reaching out to as many prominent ministers as he could. By November, he was ready to have an organizational meeting to put together a clear plan of action. The Convocation opened in St. George's Church in Edinburgh on Thursday 17 November. As Chalmers preached at the opening meeting he found himself speaking to four hundred and sixty-five ministers, a significant portion of the entire church. While there were no official minutes taken of the Convocation, it is possible to piece together what took place from the diaries and letters of Chalmers and the other participants.

There was lively debate at the Convocation on the best way forward. The earlier divisions among the evangelicals remained, although the increasing intransigence of the courts and the government were bringing more people together. After the opening worship service, the delegates moved from St. George's Church to the less prominent Roxburgh Church where, it was hoped, there would be more privacy. Chalmers was asked to chair the Convocation. From this position, he laid out a very clear vision for the future. Everyone present was aware that they were about to take a decision that would require personal sacrifice, so Chalmers sought to calm their fears.

He told his audience that the church could be economically

viable. Chalmers argued that no minister would receive an annual stipend of less than £200, that there would be an active campaign to raise funds to build new churches and schools where they were needed, and that this would be a missionary-minded church both at home and abroad. And, to prevent anyone from thinking he was simply dreaming, he told them that this programme could all be financed through the giving of the laity and the sharing of resources. He went further and made a pledge that he would undertake personally to raise the staggering amount of £100,000 each year to support the new church. At the end of the week of meetings, four hundred and twenty-three ministers signed a statement listing all of the grievances that had been inflicted on the church at the hands of the courts and the government. Then another document was signed which stated that unless there was redress, the signatories would resign their offices in the church. This second document received three hundred and fifty-four signatures. It subsequently emerged that some participants felt intimidated by Chalmers' personality and oratory, but it is still remarkable that after a week of meetings so many were prepared to sacrifice their secure livelihoods.

In January 1843, the Government announced that they were rejecting the "Claim of Right," and further, the Court of Session declared that the 1834 Chapels Act, which had set the church extension plan in motion, was illegal. The effect was to legally abolish all of the new parishes that had been created by the church. This decision only strengthened the resolve of Chalmers and his followers. On 1 February, a second Convocation was held, which resulted in the establishment of local committees whose job it was to raise funds for what would soon be a new church. Chalmers led the Finance Committee and was able to announce by the middle of

February that in Edinburgh alone £18,550 had already been raised and that donations were flowing in at the rate of £1,000 a day! During the next two and a half months local committees were established throughout Scotland to prepare for the inevitable split. Such substantial financial backing encouraged the evangelical clergymen and by the time the General Assembly met in May, there was no turning back.

The people of Scotland, and particularly of Edinburgh, were in a high state of anticipation as the General Assembly began its meetings on 18 May 1843. In fact, as early as five o'clock in the morning, the galleries of St. Andrews Church were full with people who were waiting for the opening of the Assembly, which was due to start just before three in the afternoon. At noon the Marquess of Bute, the Lord High Commissioner, representing the Queen, set out from Holyrood Palace for the short trip to St. Giles (the high church) for the opening sermon of the Assembly. Arriving at St. Giles at 12.45 pm, the High Commissioner and his retinue along with delegates to the Assembly listened to a sermon delivered by Dr. David Welsh, the moderator of the previous General Assembly and a prominent member of the evangelical party. Welsh's sermon was based on words from Romans 14:5: "Each one should be fully convinced in his own mind." In the course of his sermon, Welsh made frequent references to the crisis in the church; it was clear that something momentous was about to happen.

Following the conclusion of his sermon, Dr. Welsh led the Assembly from St. Giles to St. Andrews Church for the work of the Assembly to begin. Just before three o'clock, the Lord High Commissioner and his party took their places. The scene that unfolded was vividly described by the journalist Hugh Miller:

Never before was there seen so crowded a General
Assembly: the number of members had been increased
beyond all precedent by the double returns; and almost
every member was in his place. The Moderator opened
the proceedings by deeply impressive prayer; but though
the silence within was complete, a Babel of tumultuary
sounds outside, and at the closed doors, expressive of the
intense anxiety of the excluded multitude, had the effect of
rendering him scarcely audible in the more distant parts
of the building. There stood beside the chair, though on
opposite sides, the meet representatives of the belligerent
parties. On the right we marked Principal (Patrick)
MacFarlan of Glasgow ... On his left stood Thomas
Chalmers, the man through whose indomitable energy and
Christian zeal two hundred churches were added to the
Establishment in little more than ten years.

The Moderator rose and addressed the House in a few
impressive sentences. There had been an infringement, he
said, on the constitution of the Church,—an infringement
so great, that they could not constitute its General
Assembly without a violation of the union between Church
and State, as now authoritatively defined and declared.
He was therefore compelled, he added, to protest against
proceeding further; and, unfolding a document which he
held in his hand, he read, in a slow and emphatic manner,
the protest of the Church. For the first few seconds, the
extreme anxiety to hear defeated its object,—the universal
hush, hush, occasioned considerably more noise than it
allayed; but the momentary confusion was succeeded by
the most unbroken silence; and the reader went on till the
impressive close of the document, when he flung it down
on the table of the House, and solemnly departed. He was

followed, at a pace's distance, by Dr Chalmers; Dr Gordon and Dr Patrick MacFarlan immediately succeeded; and then the numerous sitters on the thickly occupied benches behind filed after them, in a long unbroken line, which for several minutes together continued to thread the passage to the eastern door, till at length only a blank space remained. As the well-known faces and forms of some of the ablest and most eminent men that ever adorned the Church of Scotland glided along in the current, to disappear from the courts of the State institution for ever, there rose a cheer from the galleries, and an impatient cry of "Out, out," from the ministers and elders not members of Assembly, now engaged in sallying forth, to join with them, from the railed area behind.[4]

Those leaving the Church of Scotland gathered at Tanfield Hall and Thomas Chalmers was quickly elected as the first moderator of the Free Church. He began by calling upon all those assembled to sing part of Psalm 63 from the Scottish Psalter. Contemporary accounts record that a sudden burst of light filled the building as the Assembly sang the words:

O send thy light forth and thy truth;
   Let them be guides to me,
And bring me to thine holy hill,
   E'vn where thy dwellings be.

Whether or not we accept the historical accuracy of the burst of sunlight, there is no doubt that there was a very positive mood among those who had left the Church of Scotland. The excitement of the moment, may briefly have masked the huge challenges which loomed over the fledgling denomination. By leaving the Church of Scotland, ministers lost their stipends and homes, and congregations lost their

church buildings and schools. As a result, financial matters were a main priority before the Assembly as it began its work.

In his carefully prepared moderator's address, Chalmers was quick to point out that Scotland had not witnessed a division in the church because of theological differences. While it was true that most of those gathered in Tanfield Hall were from the evangelical party, this was a breach forced on the church by the encroachment of the state and the courts on the rights of the church. It was a breaking of the relationship between the Church of Scotland and the state, because the state had broken its promises to maintain the spiritual independence of the church. Chalmers acknowledged that all those who were forming the new church were making very real sacrifices. He told the ministers, elders and supporters of the church that:

> ... it is well that you should have been strengthened by your Master in Heaven to make the surrender you have done, of everything that is dear to nature; casting aside all your earthly dependence rather than offend conscience, or incur the guilt of sinful compliance by thwarting your own sense of duty, and running counter to the Bible, our Great Church Directory and Statute Book. It is well that you have made, for the present, a clean escape from this condemnation—and that in the issue of the contest between a sacrifice of principle and a sacrifice of your worldly possessions, you have resolved upon the latter; and while to the eye of sense you are without a provision and a home, embarked upon a wide ocean of uncertainty, save that great and generous certainty which is apprehended by the eye of faith — that God reigneth, and that He will not forsake the families of the faithful.[5]

While the Assembly squarely confronted the practical

challenges the church was facing, much energy and discussion had to do with how best it could carry forward the mission of the church: to bring the gospel to Scotland and, through its foreign mission agencies, take the gospel to the rest of the world.

Although the Free Church was setting off in uncharted waters, Chalmers wanted everyone to know that he and the new church remained a staunch supporter of the establishment principle. His speech continued with these words:

> The Voluntaries mistake us, if they conceive us to be Voluntaries. We hold by the duty of the Government to give of their resources and their means for the maintenance of a Gospel in the land; and we pray that their eyes may be opened, so that they may learn how to acquit themselves as the protector of the Church and not as its corruptors or its tyrants. We pray that the sin ... into which they have fallen, may be forgiven them, and that those days of light and blessedness may speedily arrive when 'kings shall be the nursing-fathers, and queens the nursing-mothers' of our Zion. In a word, we hold that every part and function of a commonwealth should be leavened with Christianity, and that every functionary, from the highest to the lowest, should, in their respective spheres, do all that in them lies to countenance and uphold it. That is to say, though we quit the Establishment, we go out on the Establishment principle; we quit a vitiated Establishment, but would rejoice in returning to a pure one. To express it otherwise— we are the advocates for a national recognition and national support of religion—and we are not Voluntaries.[6]

Chalmers' words instilled confidence in those who were

present. Without his leadership in the years leading to 1843, it is unlikely that the evangelicals within the Church of Scotland would have been willing to take such personal risks.

Chapter 9
The Free Church 1843–1847

Thomas Chalmers was an interesting combination of the romantic and the realist. His romanticism sometimes caused him to be far too optimistic about what was achievable in his own life and ministry, but as the Free Church was launched, he looked upon the work that needed to be done in a very realistic way. Providing funds for stipends and for church building projects was the immediate need, and so as the Assembly rose from its work, prominent ministers from the Free Church undertook fundraising tours in England, Ireland and as far afield as Canada and the United States.

Chalmers assumed that the initial enthusiasm created by the Disruption would, in all likelihood, provide the necessary funds for buildings and perhaps even for pastoral stipends for a time. But after the initial enthusiasm had worn off, then what? By separating from the established church, the Free Church had, in effect, turned itself into a church that was based on voluntary contributions. This was anathema to Chalmers' belief in the establishment principle and his vision of the godly commonwealth, in which the state should be providing support for the work of the church. However, as we have seen, they believed they had no choice but to take this action. Given the circumstances, Chalmers, Charles Cowan and others had planned for what they called "the Sustentation Fund." This was the fund which had been discussed at the Convocation in November of 1842, and which was set up to help pay for stipends for clergy. It was designed so that each congregation would have a role to play in the financial stability of the whole church.

In order for the fund to work, each year local congregations collected as much money as they could for the work of the entire church. These collections were then sent to Edinburgh four times a year, where they were invested. Then, on an annual basis, every minister was paid an equal amount from the fund, which guaranteed that a basic stipend was provided for all clergy. In 1844, one year after the formation of the Free Church, the Sustentation Fund had collected £68,000 which provided a basic stipend of £100 to nearly six hundred ministers. The stipend was half of what Chalmers had originally thought it would be and in many situations in poorer areas, it was insufficient to support the work of the church. Local congregations were free to give additional amounts to their minister, and this was possible in many parishes, although these amounts varied considerably. With the combined generosity of local churches and the help of the Sustentation Fund, it was possible for some ministers to at least equal the stipends they had received prior to 1843. There was one final component to the Sustentation Fund. Not all of the money collected each year was spent. A proportion was kept back and then invested in church extension so that the church could continue to grow and meet the needs of the people of Scotland.

In the immediate period following the Disruption Chalmers believed that his talents could best be used by spreading word of the church's needs at home, so he set off on a frenetic tour of Scotland to raise support. During August and September of 1843, he visited a number of places where he knew there were supporters of the cause, who could themselves either provide needed funds or who had the necessary connections to raise money. While local committees had been hard at work raising funds before the Disruption, there was still a lot of money needed.

Chalmers correctly recognized that the first duty of the Free Church was to provide for church buildings, ministers and pastoral care for all those who associated themselves with the new church. By May 1843 there was a total amount of £76,253 in the building fund and it was used as seed money, providing at least twenty per cent of the funds needed for the construction of new church buildings. Chalmers was content to leave most of the work involving this building boom to other people. Where he did become involved was in cases where local landowners were unsympathetic to the Free Church, and who therefore were unwilling to either sell or give land for new church buildings. When faced with this problem, Chalmers used all of his connections and powers of persuasion to try and obtain suitable sites.

Both ministers and congregations leaving the Church of Scotland suffered pain and loss. The most difficult problems were experienced by those in the Highlands of Scotland and in other rural areas. Where sites for churches were not forthcoming, it was not uncommon to find groups of Christians meeting for worship in makeshift situations, and many congregations were forced, for a time, to worship in the open air. Despite these difficulties, there was amazing progress. Buildings were being erected at a remarkably fast pace, in part because of the generosity of some local businessmen who were supporters of the Free Church, and also through the donation of free labour from a number of tradesmen. Just one year after the Disruption, four hundred and seventy buildings were completed and within four years, the number had risen to seven hundred and thirty. As well as erecting new churches, the Free Church also went to court to try to recover some lost property. They did have some success regaining control of buildings which had been opened during the church extension campaign. One of the side benefits of the building programme was its positive impact on the Scottish economy. In the years immediately prior to the Disruption, there had been little building taking place, so all of the activity surrounding the new construction actually helped to lower unemployment.

Providing education for the people of Scotland was also a key component of Chalmers' strategy for the Free Church. He recognized that unless parish schools were established, many children would be left attending schools that were still connected with the Church of Scotland. Chalmers was concerned that if this situation was allowed to continue, children from Free Church homes would not understand where their church came from and why the principles it had stood for were important. At the same time there were teachers in Church of Scotland parish schools who, having expressed support for the Free Church, were losing their jobs. As a result a national education strategy was needed. At a meeting of the Assembly in October of 1843, a proposal was put forward to raise £50,000 which would be used to provide stipends for teachers and construct schools in as many parishes as possible. While this was not Chalmers' idea, he was happy to support it. To some at the Assembly, this seemed an overly optimistic target. But again, the people of Scotland demonstrated by their generosity, just how deep their support for the Free Church was. Six months later, the collection had reached a total of £52,000 and a permanent Education Fund was established. Within four years of the start of this project, there were in the region of 44,000 children attending Free Church Schools with five hundred and thirteen teachers receiving stipends.

There was also real need for the church to provide for the education of its ministers, so even before the first General Assembly, a committee was put in place to plan for a seminary. Thomas Chalmers, who had resigned his position at the University of Edinburgh when the Disruption took place, was named Principal and Senior Professor of Theology. By November of 1843, the Education Committee had secured rooms at 80 George Street in Edinburgh and one hundred and sixty-eight students enrolled in the new seminary. These rooms were seen as a temporary measure, and soon much larger plans were in place to build a permanent college that would provide instruction in the arts as well as theology. When Chalmers laid the foundation stone for "New College" on 4 June 1846 he told the assembled audience that the college would produce students who had excellent qualifications for the gospel ministry and would equip them to hold places at the very top of society. But he went on to say that what was really wanted and needed, were humble ministers who would be willing to spend time with the poorest members of their parishes and sit beside them as they died. Chalmers' point was that the education offered at the college was not an end in itself; rather it was there to help prepare men for as wide a sphere of gospel service as possible.

While much of Chalmers' time was spent on helping to raise funds for the Free Church and his teaching of divinity students, he still had energy to become involved in other projects. The first of these was his efforts in pursuit of Christian unity. It may seem odd that he would have been interested in this, given that he had just led a movement out of the Church of Scotland, but Chalmers had an expansive vision for greater unity among Christians. As we saw with reference to his pastoral work in Glasgow, Chalmers was willing to work with like-minded people from other churches to achieve his vision of the "godly commonwealth" in Scotland. He had friendships with people across denominational divides and believed in toleration among Christians as demonstrated in his involvement in the debates over Catholic emancipation. He told the first General Assembly of the Free Church that there was a real need "for the most entire co-operation" with other evangelical churches and said that the success of the progress of the gospel would "hinge not merely upon ostensible, but upon real and vital union among Christians."[1]

To achieve this, Chalmers was even prepared to acknowledge that there was no absolute scriptural definition of what form church government should take. He was content to be a Presbyterian, but he could conceive of a world where denominational differences, based on the form of government, would be less important. He was not suggesting that doctrine didn't matter but he didn't want to elevate this issue to the point where it was an absolute bar to fellowship and cooperation. At the meetings held in July of 1843 to commemorate the bicentennial of the Westminster Confession, he called for "co-operation now, and this with a view, as soon as may be, to incorporation afterwards."[2] In

1844 a book entitled *Essays on Christian Union* included an essay by Chalmers. In it he returned to this theme.

> If one in theology, we might co-operate in a thousand different ways; but we must be one in government ere we can incorporate. But if the latter obstacle do not prevent the one, let us cherish the hope that it will not long stand in the way of the other. Would that the whole Independency, and perhaps some of the Episcopacy, of Scotland, could be prevailed on to resign those external peculiarities by which we are separated; for in soul and substance, or in all the inner and essential characteristics of the faith, they seem most thoroughly at one with us. At all events, it is Presbytery which forms the great bulk and body of our various denominations. And it is a grave question, in what way the incorporation between these should be effected—whether by a corporate movement on the part of each of the uniting bodies, or by separate congregations being left to merge individually into one or other of them. Let us pray for more light, and wait the further leadings of Providence, ere we decide upon this question. And meanwhile may the spirit of love prevail over us, and keep at a distance those unseemly contentions which have brought such grievous dishonour on the Christian name, and been the plague of the church in all ages.[3]

Chalmers can be accused of being naïve on this issue, but he was motivated by a genuine desire to see the gospel impact the world. He also rightly understood that the need was great and that the more people involved in the work the better.

Although Chalmers was incredibly busy, he still enjoyed time with his daughters. William Hanna recounts that after

> ... some of his great public appearances, when he came

home exhausted, his daughters would gather round him as he lay at ease in his arm-chair. One would play Scotch music, another shampoo his feet, (a very frequent, and to him always a very agreeable operation,) a third would talk nonsense, and set him into fits of laughter. At such times, in a mock heroic way, he would repeat Scott's lines, — "O woman, in our hours of ease …". A spirit of chivalry ran through all his intercourse with his daughters: they not only ministered to his comfort in the hours of relaxation, he made them companions, as it were, of his public life, and sought their intellectual sympathy with his even highest exercises of thought.[4]

After some of his daughters married, he continued to be involved in their lives through visiting and also through regular letter writing to them. As his grandchildren were born, he delighted in them too. While always concerned about their education and spiritual welfare he was also that kind of grandfather who took time to amuse and entertain. In a letter to his grandson Tommy Hanna he talked about finding a book for him.

My dearest Tommy,—When I arrived in Edinburgh yesterday I first went to the library, and got out a very amusing book for you—Gulliver's Travels. It is not a true history, but just a story, or stories, made for the reader's entertainment.[5]

Then on another occasion, he told Tommy how much he would have liked to watch trains with him.

I wish you had been at Craigholm with us, where I lately spent three weeks. The railroad cuts the green into two parts not far from our house. But we can go from the one part to the other under an arch, and I should like to stand

in that arch with you at the time when the steam-engine
and all the carriages are passing and rattling over our
heads.[6]

The picture that emerges is of a family man who was as
concerned for their happiness and welfare, as much as he was
about the great issues of his time.

The last great project of Chalmers' life, "the West Port
Experiment" was one of the ways he attempted to put his
views on united Christian action into effect. Even though it
had been many years since he had been involved in active
pastoral ministry, he was still committed to parish ministry
and church extension. This project was begun partly as a
response to the Royal Commission that had been established
in 1843 by the British Parliament to examine the operation
of the poor laws in Scotland. Poor laws had existed in
Scotland since the fifteenth century. These laws had made a
distinction between the able bodied and those who through
age or disability were unable to work. In the sixteenth
century, individual parishes were made responsible for the
poor who lived within their boundaries. This system would
remain in place into the nineteenth century. But with poverty
increasing, the problems were much too great for the church
to contend with, and so pressure was growing for the state to
take on a much larger role in poor relief. What Chalmers was
most concerned to avoid, was the system in place in England
where poor houses held many people in squalid conditions.
He once passionately argued that voluntary gifts raised from
the generosity of Christians and distributed by the church was
the best way to alleviate poverty. He went on to say that he
wanted:

... no other asylum for our aged parents than that of their

pious and affectionate families. We can neither suffer them,
nor do we like the prospect for ourselves, of pining out the
cheerless evening of our days away from the endearments
of a home. We wish to do as long as we can without the
apparatus of English laws and English work-houses; and
should like to ward forever from our doors the system that
would bring an everlasting interdict on the worth, and
independence, and genuine enjoyments of our peasantry.
We wish to see their venerable sires surrounded, as
heretofore, by the company and the playfulness of their
own grand-children.[7]

In the summer of 1844 Chalmers gave a series of lectures
in which he again argued that the territorial or parish system
was the most effective means of helping those in society
who were most in need. Despite the fact that the Glasgow
experiments at both the Tron and St. John's parishes had not
been entirely successful, he pressed on with his ideal.

The West Port area was poor by anyone's standards, with
a large population of paupers, the homeless and significant
problems with prostitution, but this was not the reason most
people had heard of the area. Its notoriety was due to the
appalling crimes perpetrated by the Irish criminals Burke
and Hare. In 1828 they had killed seventeen people and
then sold their cadavers to the University of Edinburgh's
medical faculty. When they were caught and put on trial, their
crimes shed a light on just how difficult life on the streets
of Scotland's capital could be. While some had questioned
whether or not the needs of the Tron and St. John's parishes in
Glasgow were as great as Chalmers had portrayed them, there
could be no doubt about the need that existed in this part of
Edinburgh.

As Chalmers began planning for this outreach effort, he intentionally chose to work with Christians from different backgrounds. He still wanted there to be a Free Church parish with a church and a school, but he recognized that the need was so great that outside help would be required. He first of all contacted the Edinburgh City Mission, which already had significant experience in the area. With their blessing, the West Port Local Society came into being, and the first meeting was held on 27 July 1844. The area was divided into twenty districts with approximately twenty families in each district. It was agreed that a survey should be taken to assess the depth of the problems and the results were not encouraging.

The survey covered four hundred and eleven families and the results showed just how big the challenge was. The population was extremely mobile, with those who were employable moving frequently to find work. Few school age children actually attended school, and church attendance was very low among both Catholics and Protestants. To say that there was no sense of community would be an understatement, and few of those surveyed saw little if any value in religious instruction. It was clear that Chalmers' ideal of Christianity lived out in the community had almost entirely vanished in the squalor.

Chalmers was able to recruit a number of "visitors" whose job it would be to visit families within a designated area. They were to become acquainted with the people, to begin to teach them moral and religious principles and to encourage a community spirit. It was not their purpose to distribute charity, but they were to help in other specific ways. For example, they were told to help the unemployed find work and young people to begin apprenticeships. They were also to lobby the town council to close the many taverns and to bring other social problems to the attention of local authorities.

Work in the West Port area was slow and difficult. It was hard to find enough visitors to work directly with the people who needed help the most. Because crime rates were high, it wasn't safe for individuals to undertake the visitations alone. Chalmers' plan therefore depended on building teams of two people who would work together. The teams then met on a weekly basis to discuss progress and plan strategy. Chalmers' role in the earliest stages of the project was different from the approach he had taken in Glasgow, where he had overseen every detail of the work. Now he took a more hands-off approach so that he would not be accused of making every project dependent on his personal involvement.

One of the early workers in the West Port was William King (1812–1895). Born in Ireland, he and his family moved to the United States when he was twenty years old. Then, sensing the call to pastoral ministry, he moved to Scotland and was in the first class of students at New College following the Disruption. He would subsequently return to North America and, as a convinced abolitionist, would be involved in the underground railroad and the establishment of a community for freed slaves in Canada. His autobiography describes the conditions faced by the visitors to the West Port area as they began their work.

> The boys collected from the Street … were in such a state of filth and rags that their bodies had to be washed and their hair cut before they were set on benches. Two baths were prepared in connection with the School one for the boys and another for the girls, with a proper person to superintend each … At first not more than forty or fifty

of the adult population could be got out to Church on Sabbath, the excuse being that they had no proper clothing to go to church with.[8]

Worship services began in December of 1844 and the following April, Chalmers persuaded one of his best students William Tasker (1811–1879) to become the pastor of the West Port Free Church. Tasker had been a school teacher before entering seminary and had also worked as a home missionary in Glasgow. With his appointment, work in the West Port area picked up momentum. Soon Tasker was conducting three worship services every Sunday and threw himself into the visitation that Chalmers believed was central to the success of the project. In addition to the worship services and the school, a library, a laundry and a savings bank were opened and there were some signs that progress was being made. It is worth noting that the school was heavily subsidized but did charge fees. Chalmers believed that there would be greater ownership by parents if they were contributing financially to the education of their children. Securing funding to subsidize the work remained a priority, and this was helped by Chalmers' occasional preaching in the new congregation, which drew large crowds. Funding was also supplied by the Sustentation Fund and from wealthy philanthropists from as far away as New York City.

Chalmers preached regularly in the West Port area as the work was being established. Accounts of his sermons indicate that he frequently focused his messages on the need for repentance from sin and commitment to Christ. Recognizing that there were tensions because of the prevailing social conditions, he called on people to live together in harmony. At the conclusion of one sermon he offered this prayer:

We pray that we may be carried safely through this anxious
and distressing pilgrimage.

And we pray for a harmonized commonwealth—may the
rich and the poor know each other better, and learn to love
each other more.[9]

He had a real sense of satisfaction when in February of 1847
the West Port Territorial Church was received into the Free
Church of Scotland, and William Tasker was ordained to the
Free Church ministry. With some justification, Chalmers
could look on this congregation, which he had helped to plan,
but which others had largely carried out, as evidence that his
territorial model of ministry could work.

While there's no question that the West Port experiment did
make a significant difference to the lives of many people, it
would be too much to say that it had permanently solved the
problems which made the West Port such an impoverished
area of Edinburgh. Some have claimed that the inability to fix
the systemic problem demonstrates that Chalmers' model was
wrong. Instead, it is better to see that the social problems were
so enormous, that no one congregation or denomination,
however successful, could possibly fix them.

During the period 1845–1847 Chalmers spent considerable
energy trying to raise interest in and support for his vision for
territorial ministry in Scotland. He travelled, spoke and wrote
as much as he could in an attempt to show that the West
Port experiment was making progress and could be made to
work. Sadly, his vision for interdenominational cooperation
never got off the ground, and the funds necessary to multiply
the kind of work that had begun in the West Port were not
forthcoming.

The widespread famines of 1845 and 1846 placed considerable strain upon both church and state as they struggled to meet a very real need. First, in 1845, the potato crop failed in Ireland and then in 1846, the failure was even more widespread. In the autumn of 1846, Chalmers was instrumental in raising more than £15,000 from within the Free Church for famine relief, which placed the Free Church at the forefront of relief efforts. By early 1847, the situation was made even worse with the outbreak of typhoid. It was clear that private philanthropy, either from individuals or churches, could not meet the need. There were calls among some to let the epidemic run its course. This appalling lack of concern was based on the bizarre idea that moral failure of the inhabitants of the affected areas of Ireland and the Highlands of Scotland had brought on the famine and the plague. Chalmers angrily denounced this unfeeling attitude in a letter published in *The Witness* on 6 March 1847. Chalmers bluntly called these attitudes unchristian. Rather than spending time blaming the poor for this terrible situation, Christians, he argued, should be doing all that they could to alleviate the distress.

Then, in what can only be seen as a major change in his views, Chalmers argued in an article for the May 1847 issue of *The North British Review*, that a crisis of the proportions that was currently being faced, could only be dealt with if there was direct government intervention.

What may suffice in ordinary [situations], clearly will not suffice for the present overwhelming visitation. There is an imperious call for the Government to come forward—and this not to supersede the liberalities of the public, but to … add thereto the allowances of the State; or rather, for the State to be the principal almoner in such a dire emergency, and its distributions supplemented to the uttermost by the charities of the benevolent.[10]

He also argued that if this meant increased taxation on the wealthier in society, then the government should take this action. It has been argued that this is evidence that Chalmers was completely abandoning his ideal of the godly commonwealth. This is an overstatement. It is better to see Chalmers' views being adapted to a moment of crisis in Ireland and Scotland and a recognition that the church could not herself deal with the crisis without assistance.

In May 1847 Chalmers visited London. He had gone there to appear before a parliamentary committee, which was investigating the difficulties some Free Church congregations were experiencing in obtaining proper sites for churches. Four years after the Disruption, there were still many landowners who had neither forgiven nor forgotten, and who were going out of their way to make life as difficult as possible for the Free Church. Sir James Graham (1792–1862) took the opportunity to aggressively question Chalmers on the very existence of the Free Church, hoping to force Chalmers into conceding that the Disruption had been wrong. But Chalmers held his ground. He used the rest of his time in London to visit a number of friends and relatives and he continued to visit various people in England on his return journey to Scotland. But the visit had taken a toll on his health. He returned to Scotland clearly exhausted and many of his family and friends expressed concern for his wellbeing.

On Sunday 30 May he attended church as usual but went to bed early that night after leading family worship. When his housekeeper went to wake him the next morning as he was late for an appointment, he was found dead in his bed, having died of a heart attack sometime in the night. Thomas Chalmers was sixty-seven years old.

The grief expressed at the death of Thomas Chalmers was deep and genuine. There was a very real sense that someone important had died. As the Free Church's General Assembly was in session at the time of Chalmers' death, Edinburgh was filled with ministers and elders from all over Scotland so that when the day of the funeral came, there were many people who wanted to attend the ceremony.

The funeral took place on Friday 4 June and the *Scotsman* newspaper, which was not always sympathetic to Chalmers, commented that there had never been a larger funeral procession in the entire history of Edinburgh. Private devotions were held at the Chalmers home beginning at noon and, while this was taking place, separate services were held at Free St. Andrew's, Free St. George's and at the newly opened New College. After the services in these various locations were completed around 1 pm, the congregations formed processions which ended up outside Chalmers' home. When the coffin was removed from the house, a much larger procession of at least 2,000 was formed for the journey to the Grange Cemetery where he was to be buried. This procession included members of the town council in full regalia, and commissioners to the Free Church's General Assembly as well as many other Free Church ministers and laity. There were also representatives of many other Scottish churches, showing the respect in which Chalmers was held. Most of the city's businesses and shops were closed for the day and the streets were lined by an estimated 100,000 people. Hugh Miller's newspaper *The Witness* summarized the events when it wrote that the day's proceedings:

... spoke more emphatically than by words, of the dignity of intrinsic excellence, and of the height to which a true man may attain. It was the dust of a Presbyterian minister which the coffin contained; and yet they were burying him amid the tears of a nation, and with more than kingly honours.[11]

Chapter 10
Preacher and Leader

Thomas Chalmers was involved in active pastoral ministry for just twenty years. He was ordained in the parish of Kilmany, which he served for twelve years from 1803 until 1815 and then he pastored in Glasgow from 1815 until 1823. During his service in these churches he developed a model of ministry that was based on three principles, strong preaching, team leadership and active lay involvement. This chapter will look primarily at his sermons and touch briefly on the other two elements. Chalmers is widely regarded as one of the great preachers in the history of the Christian church. When comparing him with other preachers, Hughes Oliphant Old in his history of preaching said this:

> For those who like to speak of stars by their magnitude, Chalmers is easily in the first rank, together with Chrysostom, Spurgeon, Bernard and not many more.[1]

The early years of Chalmers' ministry in Kilmany provide a significant contrast with his later ministry. William Hanna,

· Rev. Thomas Chalmers, 1780–1847. Preacher and social reformer ·
Artist: Augustin Edouart. National Galleries of Scotland.

his sympathetic biographer and son-in-law described it in this way:

Parochial duty passed lightly upon Mr. Chalmers during his [first] seven years of ministry at Kilmany. If he expended as much effort upon the religious improvements of his people as any minister within the bounds of his presbytery ... [then] the standards to which he thus appealed, must have been miserably low ... Kindly inquiries were made, tender sympathy was shown, and needful aid was tendered; but no solicitude was manifested, as to their religious condition.[2]

Nonetheless, sermons preached during this period are still worth examining. He would take texts such as "Finally, all of you, have unity of mind, sympathy, brotherly love, a tender heart, and a humble mind" (1 Peter 3:8) and expound at great length on the subject of courteousness. Sermons like this paid scant attention to the context of the passage, or to the flow of the biblical argument. In fact, there is so little connection to the original text, we could wonder why bothered to choose it. There are few references to God and then only in the most oblique phrases such as "the benevolent Author of our frames" and there is no mention of Jesus at all.[3]

Sermons from this period were little more than lectures on morality with heavy doses of self-improvement. In this particular sermon, after explaining the value of civility to both the giver and the receiver, Chalmers said:

If civility can do so much, why in the name of tenderness, should we withhold it? Why refuse so simple an offering at the shrine of humanity? Why retire to the solitude of our own importance, and disdain to mingle in kindness with those who are brethren of the same nature and children of

the same beneficent Creator. We all sprung from heaven,
and to heaven we are all pointing.[4]

It is important to note his underlying assumptions. Everyone was essentially good and decent, and the preacher only needed to appeal to their innate goodness for society to improve. These words, although eloquently expressed, are not orthodox Christianity, and were simply expressions of pious sentiment.

While the content of this type of sermon can be questioned, it would be fair to note that as an oratorical exercise, there is something to admire. Even at this early stage of his life, Chalmers knew how to construct an argument. There was clear structure, the language was relatively simple and there was movement from stating basic premises to encouraging the hearer and reader to come to the right conclusions. This would be a feature of most of his sermons throughout his life and goes a long way to explaining the popularity of his preaching.

As we have already noted in chapter 3, Chalmers' evangelical conversion had an immediate impact on his ministry as a whole, and this can be seen in his sermons. Instead of writing them as almost an afterthought on Saturday nights, he began to spend much more time preparing during the week. His choice of texts changed, as did his prayers. The published version of a sermon based on the text Leviticus 26:34 begins with the following prayer:

> We desire, O Lord, to pay Thee the homage of our humility and of our gratitude—of our gratitude, because of the multitude of Thy mercies, and of our humility, because we are unworthy of the least of them ... Blessed be Thy name we are permitted to approach Thee. We are Thy creatures,

and have the privilege of Thy mercy. Thine all-seeing eye never abandons us—Thou hast given us a part in this wide scene of magnificence and glory—Thou hast taught us to confide in Thy goodness, and given it to feeble, wretched, sinful man to rejoice in the hand that formed, and in the right hand that guides and sustains him ... But how miserable our returns of gratitude and obedience. Alas, we have corrupted our ways—we are children of guilt and disobedience. Look, O Lord, with an eye of pity upon our weakness and upon our errors.[5]

Here we see the clear recognition of sin and the goodness and mercy of God in response to that sin. The connection between his prayers and his preaching is worth noting. Where we have a record of his prayers linked to specific sermons, they show as much thought being given to the prayer, as to the accompanying sermon.

Chalmers' method of preaching was to write a full manuscript and then, to read it to his audience, although, at some points he would abandon the prepared text. William Hanna notes that on occasion, he:

... would desert for a minute or two his manuscript, that with greater directness and familiarity of phrase, greater pointedness and personality of application, he might urge upon [his hearers] their acceptance [of] the gospel invitation.[6]

One of his parishioners said:

He would bend over the pulpit and press us to take the gift, as if he held it that moment in his hand, and would not be satisfied till every one of us had gotten possession of it. And often when the sermon was over, and the psalm was sung,

and he rose to pronounce the blessing, he would break out
afresh with some new entreaty, unwilling to let us go until
he had made one more effort to persuade us to accept it.[7]

One of the preeminent themes that emerges in his sermons
preached in Kilmany in the period immediately following his
conversion, is the greatness of the salvation offered in Christ
to the sinner.

It is not ... because you are not so great a sinner that I
would have you to be comforted; but it is because Jesus
Christ is so great a Saviour; it is not the smallness of the sin,
but the greatness of Him who died for it. I would have you
to be satisfied, but not with yourself, for this would lull you
to sleep by the administration of a poisoned opiate. I would
have you listen to that loud and widely sounding call —
"Look unto me, all ye ends of the earth, and be saved."[8]

Whether or not he was reading his manuscript, here is
passion, concern for people and a recognition that humanity's
greatest need is salvation from sin, which can only be found
in the death and resurrection of Jesus Christ.

Chalmers' reputation as a popular preacher was well
established by the time he moved to Glasgow in 1815. While
there, his *Astronomical Discourses* attracted large crowds,
and became a bestseller when they were published. As noted
earlier, the collection known as the *Tron Church Sermons*,
published in 1819 was not successful commercially, but does
provide an important insight into his theology and preaching
method. The seventeen sermons have a common theme, the
"depravity of human nature and [its] adequate and powerful
remedy" found in the good news of the gospel.[9]

To modern ears these sermons may seem at times to be

depressing and melancholic. However, they reflect the truth of Christianity that humanity is lost without Christ and is dead in trespasses and sins. Chalmers makes those points very clearly and he is equally clear that faith in Christ is the only way of escape from the problem of sin and rebellion against God. While these are not Chalmers' most famous sermons, they are essential to a proper understanding of his theology and ministry.

Another important theme in these sermons, is that those who have received Christ are changed people. Changed because of the finished and complete work of Christ and the gift of the Holy Spirit. With this knowledge the Christian can then be:

> ... a trusting, and a working, and a praying, and a rejoicing, and a trembling disciple, ... because, with a faith commensurate to the testimony of God, I give myself over in my whole mind, and whole person to the authority of a whole Bible.[10]

This theme would reappear repeatedly through the remainder of Chalmers' ministry.

Like most Scottish preachers of his time, Chalmers was an exegetical preacher, who spent periods of his ministry working through Scripture in an orderly way. The principal example of this is the series of one hundred sermons on the Epistle to the Romans, most of which were preached while he was the minister at St. John's. These sermons, which were subsequently published as *Lectures on Romans*, give a glimpse of both the method and content of his preaching.[11] There is detailed exegesis of the epistle combined with real evangelistic fervour.

If God spared not His own Son to reconcile a world
that had nothing but guilt and depravity to offer to His
contemplation—how much more, now that atonement is
made, will He bless and enrich all those who have fled to
it for refuge, and whom He now beholds in the face of His
anointed. This then is an argument altogether addressed
to the hope of faith, and may be seized upon and felt in
the whole force of it, ere there is time for the hope of
experience. The moment that one looks with a believing
eye to the work of redemption, he may gather from it all
the materials which make up this argument. He may there
see, that Christ at that time died for the sinful, to bring
about their agreement with God; and that, at the present
time, Christ has not to die any more, and that in Him the
guilt of sinfulness has been done away. 'If when enemies
we were reconciled, by His death—how much more, now
that we are reconciled, shall all the blessings that He died to
purchase be lavished upon us abundantly.'[12]

It is notable that when Chalmers is preaching on Romans
9:3, which touches on the doctrine of election, his main
emphasis is to remind his hearers that the gospel is freely
offered to all. He states that while it:

… is most true that God has the power over human hearts,
to turn them whithersoever He will; and if demanded why
then do not all the hearts of men receive that touch from
the hands of His omnipotence which might turn them unto
the way of life, our reply is still that we cannot say. But this
we are empowered to say, that there is not a hard-hearted
sinner amongst you, who is not within the scope of the
invitation. Come ye also and be saved; and to your prayers
for the clean heart and the right spirit, a softening and a
sanctifying influence will be made to descend upon you.[13]

Another important feature of Chalmers' sermons on Romans is their confident expectation that the gospel would spread throughout the world. This reflected his eschatology which was post-millennial in nature.[14] In coming to this understanding, he was following a long-established understanding in the Protestant tradition which looked forward to the spread of the gospel throughout the earth and a period of great blessing before the second coming of Christ. This view was popularized in the marginal notes found in the Geneva Bible of 1599 and can also be found in many of the Puritans and their successors in both England and Scotland, as well as in Jonathan Edwards in America.[15]

It is important to note here that this post-millennialism must not be confused with the school of thought known as theonomy or Christian Reconstructionism, which was popularized in America in the twentieth century. Thomas Chalmers and the Disruption-era Free Church were not interested in a Christianity that was forced on society through the radical imposition of Old Testament civil law. Rather, Chalmers believed that the gospel had the power to transform nations and cultures as people came to saving faith in Christ and lived out their faith in the world.

Post-millennial exegesis of Romans 11 typically taught that the Jews would come to faith in Christ, which would in turn, have a massive impact on the growth of the whole church. Chalmers followed this exegetical tradition in his sermon on Romans 11:26 "And so all Israel shall be saved." Here he stated that the conversion of the Jews to Christianity:

> ... will be followed up by a mighty enlargement in the character and state of Christianity throughout the world— so that in labouring for this, we become in a peculiar

manner the fellow-workers of God, and instruments in His
hand, for prosecuting and carrying forward to its fulfilment
one of the highest objects of His administration ... It [is]
the most germinant of all our missionary enterprises—or
the one most prolific of a rich moral blessing to the great
family of mankind. The full return of the Jews will be the
riches, we are told, of all other nations.[16]

It is also noteworthy that Chalmers was deeply concerned
about how badly much of Christendom had treated the Jews
throughout history, and so he called on the church to:

... turn from the evil of our way towards them and mourn
over all the insults and the wrongs which for two thousand
years have been heaped on this people of noble ancestry
and of still nobler destination.[17]

Chalmers' optimistic eschatology provided an impetus for
much of what he did and helped him to keep moving forward
in his life, when challenges came his way.

Arguably the best-known sermon by Thomas Chalmers,
was one based on words from 1 John 2:15, "love not the world,
neither the things that are in the world. If any man love
the world, the love of the Father is not in him." Chalmers
preached "The Expulsive Power of a New Affection" while he
was pastor of St. John's parish church in Glasgow. The sermon
marks another stark contrast with the moralism he preached
in the early years of his ministry. Here he argues, that what is
commanded in the text is something that cannot take place
without the supernatural grace of God.

To bid a man into whom there has not yet entered the great
and ascendant influence of the principle of regeneration,
to bid him withdraw his love from all the things that are in

the world, is to bid him give up all the affections that are in his heart. The world is the all of a natural man. He has not a taste nor a desire that points not to a something placed within the confines of its visible horizon. He loves nothing above it, and he cares for nothing beyond it; and to bid him love not the world, is to pass a sentence of expulsion on all the inmates of his bosom.[18]

Chalmers went on;

The love of God and the love of the world, are two affections, not merely in a state of rivalship, but in a state of enmity — and that so irreconcilable, that they cannot dwell together in the same bosom. We have already affirmed how impossible it were for the heart, by any innate elasticity of its own, to cast the world away from it; and thus reduce itself to a wilderness. The heart is not so constituted; and the only way to dispossess it of an old affection, is by the expulsive power of a new one.[19]

This love of God comes as a free gift and:

… never does the sinner find within himself so mighty a moral transformation, as when under the belief that he is saved by grace, he feels constrained thereby to offer his heart a devoted thing, and to deny ungodliness.[20]

It would be too strong to say that this was the most important sermon that Chalmers ever preached, but it does reflect the heart of his ministry. He believed that it was only the good news of the gospel, given in God's authoritative revelation in Scripture, that could provide hope for humanity, and that had the power to transform individual lives and the life of the nation.

A survey of Chalmers' published sermons, shows a man

whose preaching ministry encompassed an extremely wide
variety of topics. In the biographical chapters we have already
noted some of the issues that he addressed from his pulpit,
and a few more examples will suffice to show the breadth
of his interests. In 1820, at a time of some national unrest,
he preached a sermon on Romans 3:9–19 entitled "The
Importance of Civil Government in Society." Accepting as
he did the establishment principle, Chalmers held firmly to
the belief that both the church and the state were divinely
appointed institutions with God-given responsibilities. As
he looked at the problems facing Scotland and the evils that
threatened stability, Chalmers boldly stated that God has
established civil government "for the church's good upon
earth."[21] At the same time, Chalmers did not for a moment
believe that civil government and the absence of anarchy
would automatically make for a healthy society. Increased
levels of education overseen by the church were needed, but
primarily what was required, was that the good news of the
gospel should be preached.

> Let us go forth, without restraint, on the work of
> evangelizing the world, and the world, under such a
> process, will become the blissful abode of Christian and
> well-ordered families. And let us go forth, with equal
> alacrity, to the work of spreading education among our own
> people ... The growth of intelligence and of moral worth
> among the people, will at length stamp upon them all that
> majesty of which they will ever be ambitious; and, instead
> of a precarious tranquility, resting upon the basis of an
> ignorance ever open to the influences of delusion, will the
> elements of peace, and truth, and righteousness, be seen to
> multiply along with the progress of learning in our land.[22]

The same man who could preach at length on civil

government and the proper ordering of society, also preached sermons on animal welfare. On 5 March 1826 he preached a sermon based on a text in Proverbs 12:19 "a righteous man regardeth the life of his beast." His principal point in the sermon was to remind his hearers that God had condescended to bring salvation to the world and as a result, there is warrant for caring for His creation.

> He who hath given his angels charge concerning us, means that the tide of beneficence should pass from order to order, through all the ranks of his magnificent creation; and we ask, is it with man that this goodly provision is to terminate—or shall he, with all his sensations of present blessedness, and all his visions of future glory let down upon him from above, shall he turn him selfishly and scornfully away from the rights of those creatures whom God hath placed in dependence under him?[23]

Sermons like this one do not always provide the best examples of exegesis and some of his more topical messages seem overly complex and meandering. But no pastor preaches an excellent sermon every week, and Chalmers' weaker efforts do not detract from the fact that his pulpit ministry was hugely influential and richly blessed.

While Chalmers' sermons were central to his work as a minister, there were other key elements that also characterized his pastoral work. The first of these was team leadership. As we saw in Chapter 4, when he arrived in Glasgow, he undertook to visit as much of the Tron parish as he possibly could. As he did so, he came to recognize that the work of evangelization and caring for the poor could not be done without help. So, while Chalmers was the face of the churches he led, a lot of work in the parish was done by the elders and deacons. And it went further than this. He also cultivated, cajoled and challenged every Christian in the church to become involved.

The principal method he used at both the Tron and St. John's was the development of Sabbath Schools and lay visitation. As he recruited people to this work, he faced some challenges. William Hanna described the opposition in this way:

> It was not, however, upon a flowing tide of approval or popularity that these Sabbath-school operations at the commencement moved. It was very much the reverse. There were indeed a few, who from the very beginning hailed them with delight. But over the general public of Glasgow the spirit of religious indifference as yet strongly prevailed. That spirit looked upon such efforts with cold dislike, and when stirred into quicker life by such energy as was now embarked in their prosecution, it kindled into a disdainful opposition, and tried to fill its mouth with arguments. These Sabbath-schools, it was said, would interfere with the proper domestic training of the young. They were engaging laymen in what was fit and suitable employment for clergymen alone.[24]

The opposition to having laymen do work that was "fit and suitable for clergymen alone" struck at the heart of what Chalmers was attempting to develop and achieve, and he was quick to come to its defense. This he did by stressing the magnitude of the problem.

> I feel as if it were a mighty and impenetrable mass, truly beyond the strength of one individual arm, and before which, after a few furtive and unavailing exertions, nothing remains but to sit down in the idleness of despair. It is a

number, it is a magnitude, it is an endless succession of houses and families ... it is an utter impossibility, even with the most active process of [pastoral] visitation to meet the ever-pressing demands of the sick, and the desolate and the dying, — it is all this, I confess, which tempts me to seek for relief in some wise and efficient system of deputation. In these circumstances I do feel greatly obliged by every contribution to the great cause ... I rejoice particularly in the multiplication of those humble and often despised [schools] ... I am certain that they are well suited to the present needs and circumstances of our population.[25]

In November of 1845 Chalmers returned to this theme in his Principal's Address to students at New College. While making no excuse for requiring his theological students to follow an intense course of instruction, he went on to say that the work of the church also depended on active participation from the laity.

There are offices besides that of ordained minister ... there are other directions for Christian philanthropy besides, which I should like to see occupied in tens and fifties and hundreds by the religious and intelligent laymen of our church, that a varied and extensive agency may arise in the midst of us fully equipped for the work, and girded for a strenuous and determined warfare against the irreligion and profligacy of our age.[26]

As work began in the West Port area Chalmers went so far as to say that the only hope of success would be through the active support of the laity.

We shall never be able to make a great impression, unless we avail ourselves of the lay part of the people: and many there are who, though they have not received the advantage of a University education, and are not accustomed to public speaking, yet, feeling the love of Christ in their hearts, are able to go forth to collect a few people in a room, and perform the Sabbath services in the midst of them.[27]

When people today reflect on Chalmers' influence, they rightly emphasize the impact of his preaching and his reinvigoration of the offices of elder and deacon. But without this vision for reaching the lost and needy by means of mobilizing the laity, he would not have achieved as much as he did.

Chapter 11
Chief Scottish Man

In the weeks following Chalmers' death, many memorial services were held throughout Scotland amid feelings that the country and the church would never be quite the same again. Tributes to his life and work flowed in from all over Scotland, England and North America. The *Spectator*, published in London, commented on his death in this way:

> It is not often that a man can be said to have "lived all his days," so truly as in the case of Thomas Chalmers. The oldest reminiscences of him that have been preserved, present the image of a young and ardent spirit luxuriating in the exercise of its powers, scarcely able to confine itself within the conventional sphere of activity prescribed to those of the profession which was nevertheless of all within his reach the best suited to his tastes and faculties: and he has been taken away while still earnestly toiling in his vocation, before any symptoms of mental weakness or of lassitude and aversion to work had become visible.[1]

While the *Spectator* then went on to question some of

THOMAS CHALMERS, D.D. LL.D.

•　Thomas Chalmers in old age　•

Chalmers ideas and accomplishments, they generously concluded their obituary with these words.

> His earnest benevolence ... was contagious. He was the
> Socrates of the school of Christian pastors he has founded:
> the value and importance of what he taught will be more
> apparent in the intellects he has formed than in any work
> he has left us.[2]

Given the passage of time since the death of Thomas Chalmers, it is appropriate that we should ask what his significance is for today, both positively and negatively.

Thomas Chalmers was, first and foremost, committed to the local church. After his conversion, God used his efforts to revitalize the parish of Kilmany. Because of his preaching and pastoral care, commitment to the local church increased and Chalmers began to test his territorial model of ministry. Much has been written about his ministry in Glasgow and, it would be fair to concede, that his work at the Tron and St. John's parishes, may not have been quite as successful as Chalmers or his friends claimed it to be.

However, these churches did make a positive difference in their respective communities. Through his preaching the light of the gospel shone forth, and through the schools and the work carried out by an active diaconate, lives were changed. Chalmers clearly recognized that for the local church to progress, the work of the ministry had to be shared. His Glasgow parishes only succeeded because there were small armies of people who had caught Chalmers' vision for the church, and who were prepared to devote themselves to it wholeheartedly. This is a pattern of ministry with perpetual relevance.

We are now living in an era where the prevailing philosophy of ministry in many places appears to be that the bigger something is, the better it will necessarily be. We tend also to look to megastars to do the work. The problem with this view is that it overlooks the ministry and mission of smaller local churches which have been tasked to take the gospel to the communities where God has placed them. Chalmers always understood that if Christianity was going to transform lives, this had to happen through the presence of faithful, worshipping and caring churches in every community.

As we have seen, Chalmers spent a significant portion of his life working in academia. In doing this he understood that the academy was never an end in itself, rather it was the place where training for ministry and missionary endeavors took place. His years at St. Andrews, the University of Edinburgh and New College, helped prepare a generation of ministers and missionaries for the Free Church. He may have been teaching moral philosophy and theology to his students, but what he was really doing was communicating pastoral theology based on his many years of parish experience.

Chalmers' years in academic work also produced a vast literature on everything from economics to politics and to what we would now call sociology. We needn't necessarily embrace all of his conclusions to see that his investigations make an important point. What he showed very clearly was that Christians do not need to be afraid of the world of ideas and, in fact, the more we speak into these spheres the better off the world will be.

There is also much that can be learned from Chalmers' style of leadership. The Disruption of 1843 and the creation of the Free Church was used by God to reinvigorate the church in Scotland. The Free Church came into existence largely because Chalmers would not give in to state interference in the affairs of the church and he was able to communicate a way forward and bring many people along with him. He was not only gifted in being able to formulate and communicate a vision, he also knew how to motivate people to support it. Chalmers knew that leadership meant not only pointing in a particular direction, but also taking people step by step through the process so that they too could understand the vision and carry it out.

Chalmers was far from being a perfect leader. When he faced opposition, he could be ruthless. He tended to push forward regardless of opposition and he seems to have been unable to consider the possibility that those who disagreed with him might have something to teach him. All leaders need to be prepared to listen to the perspectives of others. It is just possible that some of the conflict Chalmers faced in his life could have been avoided had he taken more time, exercised more patience and been willing to concede that the perspectives of others could be valuable.

Our survey of the life and ministry of Thomas Chalmers has shown us a man who lived life very much in the public eye. In his early life, before his evangelical conversion, he sought publicity through his publishing and his desire to find a prestigious academic appointment. Following his conversion, it could be said that the world sought him. From the time of his move to Glasgow, he was never far from public view. In fact, to use a modern phrase, he was a public theologian, someone who engaged the issues of the day from an explicitly Christian perspective.

He was persuasive as a preacher, and he was equally powerful when he spoke on issues of public importance.

> The overriding impression of contemporaries, in an age famous for oratory, was of his brilliance as a public speaker and of his ability to sway his hearers ... "he buried his adversaries under the fragments of burning mountains", is the only image that suggests an idea of his eloquent imagination and terrible energy. He was for effect ... unapproached in our day. [3]

Sometimes, his interventions were on issues directly related to the life of the church, as he called on the state to provide proper financial support. He was also quick to defend the rights of the church against the encroachments of the state. But, as we have seen, he spoke on other issues as well, such as the proper care for the poor and disadvantaged and the need for proper support for education. Then he also engaged in purely political issues such as Roman Catholic emancipation.

Chalmers believed that one of the implications of the establishment principle was that he, and other representatives of the church, had the right, even duty, to speak truth to power. He didn't ask for permission to speak to politicians on public issues. He didn't hesitate to preach to his congregations on topics that were directly related to the issues of the day, and he also didn't wait to be invited to speak on these issues. What he did do was to put forward the best case he could on a range of issues. He wasn't always successful and didn't always achieve his goals, but he was fearless in his attempts to persuade.

It has been correctly noted that one of Chalmers' aims was to "reassert the church's role as an instrument of Christian service."[4] Through this service, he confidently expected that the church would directly impact the political and social economy of the nation. While Chalmers saw it as the church's duty to care for the poor, he also came to recognize that some problems were greater than the church could solve. He therefore believed there was a role for the state to play in relieving social ills. It would be a blessing for the church and the world if we were to embrace this element of Chalmers' vision.

We are now living in a very different time than did Chalmers. The parish system which was at the heart of so much of what he did, no longer exists in any meaningful way in most of Christendom. The church in the west is much weaker than it was and has lost much of its influence. But perhaps this weakness is in part because we have lost confidence in the power of the gospel and have become too inward looking. Chalmers would not have recognized the pessimism of many twenty-first-century Christians. Instead of lamenting the secularization of society, he would be telling us to get busy and bring the gospel to bear on every area of life.

There are too few who endorse Chalmers' understanding of the relationship between the church and the state and we are the poorer for it. But even if the establishment principle has fallen out of favour, surely there are still valuable lessons to be learned in this area. In an essay entitled "The Establishment Principle Today," the Scottish theologian Donald Macleod offered some very important guidance on how Christians should understand their role in the world. He argued that Christians need to be prepared to "expose the fallacy that secular humanism represents religious neutrality, and we must bear witness to the universal lordship of Jesus Christ."[5] Bearing witness to the lordship of Jesus Christ means that individual Christians, and the church as a whole, have a right

and a duty to speak on the important issues of the day. There
are correct biblical insights which need to be expressed and
we should be prepared to do so, even if doing this opens us up
to criticism and even persecution. Macleod also says that the:

> ... church must educate government as to those Christian
> values which should form the basis of its administration.
> The most fundamental and relevant of these is stated
> in Isaiah 61:8, 'I, the LORD, love justice' ... God is
> concerned for the rights of all his creatures, and hates to
> see them violated. This is why he is always on the side
> of the victims of injustice, and it follows from this that
> the rights of widows, orphans, aliens, immigrants, the
> sick, the unemployed, the disabled, the homeless and the
> marginalized must lie at the heart of any political witness
> borne by the church. Our voice cannot be limited to narrow
> issues of law-and-order, far less to questions of sexual
> morality. We must speak in support of the powerless and
> the speechless.[6]

Some Christians will dismiss this as being too closely
related to the social gospel as promulgated in the twentieth
century. This is untrue. Rather, it is the application of the
gospel to every area of life which Christians are called upon
to do and which Thomas Chalmers tirelessly did. Chalmers
would also have largely agreed that Christians should:

> ... speak in support of the institution of government itself.
> It is right that its work be open to criticism and review, to
> satire and even to demonstrations of public protest. But
> we must never forget that government is appointed by
> God, that its members are his servants and that it is our
> only protection against anarchy (or tyranny: there is little
> difference between them. All tyranny is anarchical). From

this point of view the church should give legitimacy to government from the word of God, bearing witness that we live under a lawful authority and that we are bound to comply with every lawful exercise of that authority.[7]

And if we live in free societies,

… we should inculcate gratitude for the specific system of government under which we live: gratitude for democratic elections which call governments to account; gratitude for the overall quality of our [politicians]; and gratitude for the public services, internal security, personal freedoms and individual prosperity we enjoy.[8]

Was Thomas Chalmers the "chief Scottish man of his time" as Thomas Carlyle stated? Or, was his life "in one sense a tragic disappointment" as Stewart J. Brown has suggested?[9] Our brief study of his life points us in the direction of seeing Chalmers as a flawed but nonetheless highly significant figure. He was responsible for a major change in the direction of the Scottish church in the nineteenth century. He was considered one of the greatest preachers of his day and many of his sermons still have the capacity to enlighten and inspire. He helped motivate and train a generation of students, many of whom went on to do significant work. His tireless efforts on behalf of the poor and underprivileged changed the way that those less fortunate were viewed and cared for. He reawakened the church to an awareness of her social responsibilities and he was an energetic spokesman for the church on issues of public interest. This is hardly a failure, and calling his life a disappointment does not do justice to his legacy.

In an age in which history is significantly devalued, it isn't surprising that many people have not heard of Thomas

Chalmers. And of those who have, some question his long-term impact. As Michael Fry has noted historians:

> ... brought up in the Scottish socialism of the late twentieth century have taken the sniffiest possible attitude to Chalmers' exertions as being at bottom motivated by dogmatic callousness ... Yet in his own time he was much admired for his depth of commitment to his work and his decision to go and live among the poor (as few modern academics would care to do). Even in the Scotland of the twenty-first century we may yet develop a more open attitude to the idea that poverty will be best treated by engagement of local communities and fellow human beings rather than by impersonal handouts from the bureaucracy of a state washing its hands of further consequence.[10]

Thomas Carlyle was correct to warn that it would be a bad thing if the world forgot Thomas Chalmers. And it has largely forgotten him. Even when he is remembered, the focus isn't always on the most important part of his life and ministry. While his leadership in the church, his views on social issues, his work as an academic and writer were all important, they were not the preeminent thing in his life. Rather, the primary focus should be on Chalmers as the pastor, who cared for his people and preached the good news about Jesus Christ. It was this good news of sins forgiven, and new life in Christ, that animated his life. Ignoring this means that we will miss what motivated him, and we will not understand the heart of his ministry.

This can best be summed up in his own words, from a sermon based on Ecclesiastes 4:13. Here Chalmers made this powerful statement about the power of the Christian gospel to change the world. The gospel, he said, is:

... the great instrument for ... elevating the poor ... Let the testimony of God be simply taken in, that on his own Son he has laid the iniquities of us all ... Jesus Christ died, the just for the unjust, to bring us unto God. This is a truth, which, when all the world shall receive it, all the world will be renovated. Many do not see how a principle, so mighty in operation, should be enveloped in a proposition so simple of utterance. But let a man, by his faith in this utterance, come to know that God is his friend, and that heaven is the home of his fondest expectation; and in contact with such new elements as these, he will evince the reach, and the habit, and the desire of a new creature. It is this doctrine which is the alone instrument of God for the moral transformation of our species.[11]

Bibliography

Anderson, John. *Reminiscences of Thomas Chalmers, D.D. LL.D.* Edinburgh: James Nichol, 1851.

Black, Alasdair. "The Balfour Declaration: Scottish Presbyterian Eschatology and British Policy Toward Palestine." *Perichoresis*, 16 no. 4 (2018), 35–59.

Brown, Stewart J. *Thomas Chalmers and the Godly Commonwealth*. Oxford: Oxford University Press, 1982.

Chalmers, Thomas. *The Application of Christianity to the Commercial and Ordinary Affairs of Life, in a Series of Discourses*. Glasgow: Chalmers & Collins, 1820.

_____ *Discourses on the Christian Revelation Viewed in Connection with Modern Astronomy. To Which are Added Discourses Illustrative of the Connection Between Theology and General Science*. New York: Robert Carter & Brothers, 1851.

_____ "Dr. Chalmers' Essay" in *Essays on Christian Union*. London: Hamilton & Adams, 1845.

_____ *Lectures on the Epistle of Paul the Apostle to the Romans. Vol. 1*. Glasgow: William Collins, 1837.

_____ *Lectures on the Epistle of Paul the Apostle to the Romans. Vol. 2.* Glasgow: William Collins, 1838.

_____ *Lectures on the Epistle of Paul the Apostle to the Romans. Vol. 3.* Glasgow: William Collins, 1840.

_____ *Lectures on the Epistle of Paul the Apostle to the Romans. Vol. 4.* Glasgow: William Collins, 1840.

_____ *Observations on a Passage in Mr. Playfair's Letter to the Lord Provost of Edinburgh Relative to the Mathematical Pretensions of the Scottish Clergy.* Cupar, Fife: R Tullis, 1867.

_____ "Political Economy of a Famine." *The North British Review.* 7 (May–Aug.1847): 247–290.

_____ *Prelictions on Butler's Analogy, Paley's Evidences of Christianity, and Hill's Lectures in Divinity.* Edinburgh: Thomas Constable and Co., 1852.

_____ *The Second Speech of Dr. Chalmers on the Catholic Question at the Presbyterian Meeting, Edinburgh April 1, 1829.* London: H.A. Arliss, 1829.

_____ *Sermons and Discourses of Thomas Chalmers, D.D., LL. D, Now Completed by the Introduction of his Posthumous Sermons.* New York: Robert Carter & Brothers, 1854.

_____ *Sermons by the Late Thomas Chalmers D.D., L.L. D., Illustrative of Different Stages in His Ministry, 1798–1847.* New York: Harper & Brothers, 1849.

_____ *Sermons, Preached in the Tron Church Glasgow by Thomas Chalmers, D.D. Minister of the Tron Church, Glasgow.* Glasgow: John Smith and Son, 1819.

Cheyne, A.C. "Introduction Thomas Chalmers: Then and Now" in *The Practical and the Pious Essays on Thomas Chalmers 1780–1847,* ed. A.C. Cheyne. Edinburgh: Saint Andrews Press, 1985.

Davis, John Jefferson. *Christ's Victorious Kingdom.* Laurel, MS: Audubon Press, 2006.

Finlayson, Sandy. *Unity and Diversity: The Founders of the Free Church of Scotland.* Fern, Ross-shire: Christian Focus, 2010.

Fry, Michael. *A New Race of Men: Scotland 1815–1914.* Edinburgh: Birlinn, 2013.

Goodell, Charles Le Roy. *Heralds of a Passion.* New York: Ray Long & Richard R. Smith, 1932.

Hanna, Anne. *Letters and Journals of Anne Chalmers, Edited by Her Daughter.* London: The Chelsea Publishing Co, 1923.

Hanna, William. *Memoirs of the Life and Writings of Thomas Chalmers.* Edinburgh: Edmonston and Douglas, 1867.

Hanna, William *Selections from the Correspondence of the Late Thomas Chalmers* Edinburgh: Thomas Constable, 1853.

Ives, Michael J. "Desert Rose, Thomas Chalmers' West Port Experiment (1844–1847)." *The Confessional Presbyterian* 14 (2018): 115–125, 268–269.

King, William. *Autobiography of Rev. William King: Written at Intervals During the Last Three Years of His Life.* Typescript, Presbyterian Church of Canada Archives, n.d.

McCaffrey, John F. "Thomas Chalmers and Social Change." *The Scottish Historical Review* LX, 1: no. 169 (April 1981): 32–60.

MacLeod, A. Donald. *A Church Disrupted: Charles Cowan MP and the Free Church of Scotland*. Fern, Ross-shire: Christian Focus, 2013.

Miller, Hugh. *Headship of Christ and the Rights of the Christian People*. Boston: Gould and Lincoln, 1863.

Old, Hughes Oliphant. *The Reading and Preaching of the Scriptures in the Worship of the Christian Church. Vol. 2, Moderatism, Pietism and Awakening*. Grand Rapids MI: Eerdmans, 2004.

Roxborogh, John. *Thomas Chalmers Enthusiast for Mission, the Christian Good of Scotland and the Rise of the Missionary Movement*. Rutherford Studies in Historical Theology Carlisle: Paternoster Publishing, 1999.

Watt, Hugh. *Thomas Chalmers and the Disruption*. Edinburgh, Thomas Nelson and Sons, 1943.

Wilberforce, William. *A Practical View of the Prevailing Religious System of Professed Christians, in the Middle and Higher Classes in this Country, Contrasted with Real Christianity*. Dublin: Robert Dapper, 1797.

Wilson, William. *Memorials of Robert Smith Candlish*. Edinburgh: Adam and Charles Black, 1880.

Endnotes

Introduction

1   William Hanna, *Memoirs of the Life and Writings of Thomas Chalmers*, (Edinburgh: Edmonston and Douglas, 1867). William Hanna (1808–1882) was married to Thomas Chalmers' eldest daughter Anne (1813–1891). He was a minister in the Church of Scotland and later the Free Church. Hanna's *Life of Thomas Chalmers* was originally published in four volumes. References in this book are to the two-volume edition that was published in 1867.

2   Thomas Carlyle, "Letter to William Hanna 7 June 1852" *The Carlyle Letters* Online https://carlyleletters.dukeupress.edu/ (accessed March 20, 2019).

Chapter 1

1   There were separate Acts passed in both Scotland and England which united the two countries.

2   John F. McCaffrey "Thomas Chalmers and Social Change," *The Scottish Historical Review*, LX, 1: no. 169 (April 1981): 40.

3   Non-conformists were Protestants who did not conform to the liturgical practices and government of the Church of England.

4   Quoted in Charles Le Roy Goodell, *Heralds of a Passion* (New York: Ray Long & Richard R. Smith, 1932), 59.

Chapter 2

1   Hanna, *Memoirs of the Life and Writings of Thomas Chalmers*, I:13

Chapter 3

1   Ibid., 61.

2   Ibid., 62–63.

3   Thomas Chalmers, *Observations on a Passage in Mr. Playfair's Letter to the Lord Provost of Edinburgh Relative to the Mathematical Pretensions of the Scottish Clergy* (Cupar-Fife: R. Tullis, 1867), 48.

4   This particularly cutting comment appeared in *The Eclectic Review*, July 1808, 576–89. Quoted in John Roxborogh Thomas Chalmers Enthusiast for Mission, the Christian Good of Scotland and the Rise of the Missionary Movement *Rutherford Studies in Historical Theology* (Carlisle: Paternoster Publishing, 1999), 18.

5   Ibid., 20.

6   Hanna, *Memoirs of the Life and Writings of Thomas Chalmers*, I:112.

7   William Wilberforce, *A Practical View of the Prevailing Religious System of Professed Christians, in the Middle and Higher Classes in this Country, Contrasted with Real Christianity* (Dublin: Robert Dapper, 1797), 82.

8   Hanna, *Memoirs of the Life and Writings of Thomas Chalmers*, I:138.

9   Quoted in Hugh Watt, *Thomas Chalmers and the Disruption* (Edinburgh, Thomas Nelson and Sons, 1943), 33.

10   At every celebration of the Lord's Supper, people who intended to receive the sacrament had to receive a token from the minister and Kirk Session, which indicated they had been examined and found fit to participate in the sacrament.

11   Anne Hanna, *Letters and Journals of Anne Chalmers, Edited by Her Daughter* (London: The Chelsea Publishing Co, 1923), 17.

12   Thomas Chalmers, *Sermons and Discourses of Thomas Chalmers, D.D., LL.D, Now Completed by the Introduction of his Posthumous Sermons* (New York: Robert Carter & Brothers, 1854) 1:495, 505.

Chapter 4

1   Thomas Chalmers, *Discourses on the Christian Revelation Viewed in Connection with Modern Astronomy. To Which are Added Discourses Illustrative of the Connection Between Theology and General Science* (New York: Robert Carter & Brothers, 1851), 88.

2   Ibid., 180.

3   Thomas Chalmers, "The Discourse of Christian Charity Applied to the Case of Religious Differences," in *Sermons and Discourses of Thomas Chalmers,* 2:246.

Chapter 5

1   A rule of thumb for monetary equivalencies is that £1 in the mid-nineteenth century is now worth approximately £100. "Inflation Calculator," Bank of England, accessed June 22, 2019, https://www.bankofengland.co.uk/monetary-policy/inflation/inflation-calculator.

2   Hanna, *Memoirs of the Life and Writings of Thomas Chalmers,* 1:566–567.

3   Thomas Chalmers, "The Application of Christianity to the Commercial and Ordinary Affairs of Life," in a *Series of Discourses* (Glasgow: Chalmers & Collins, 1820), 43–44.

4   A. C. Cheyne "Introduction Thomas Chalmers: Then and Now," in *The Practical and the Pious Essays on Thomas Chalmers 1780–1847* (Edinburgh: Saint Andrews Press, 1985), 62.

Chapter 6

1   Hanna, *Memoirs of the Life and Writings of Thomas Chalmers*, 2:148.

2   For a profile of Alexander Duff see the chapter "Alexander Duff — Pioneer Missionary" in Sandy Finlayson *Unity and Diversity: The Founders of the Free Church of Scotland* (Fearn Ross-Shire: Christian Focus, 2009), 237–260.

3   Hanna, *Memoirs of the Life and Writings of Thomas Chalmers*, 2:159.

Chapter 7

1   Ibid., 2:177.

2   Chalmers, "The Respect Due to Antiquity," in *Sermons and Discourses of Thomas Chalmers*, 1:246.

3   Thomas Chalmers, The Second Speech of Dr. Chalmers on the Catholic Question at the Presbyterian Meeting, Edinburgh April 1, 1829 (London: H.A. Arliss, 1829), 8.

4   Thomas Chalmers, "On the Death of the Rev. Dr. Andrew Thompson," in *Sermons and Discourses of Thomas Chalmers*, 1:273.

5   These new parishes were officially known as *quad sacra* parishes, which meant that they had been established by an act of the church rather than by the civil authorities.

6   William Hanna, *Selection from the Correspondence of the Late Thomas Chalmers* (Edinburgh: Thomas Constable), 339.

Chapter 8

1   For a profile of Robert Candlish see the chapter "Robert S. Candlish — Preacher and Churchman" in Sandy Finlayson, *Unity and Diversity: The Founders of the Free Church of Scotland* (Fearn Ross-Shire: Christian Focus, 2009), 59–82.

2   William Wilson, *Memorials of Robert Smith Candlish* (Edinburgh: Adam and Charles Black, 1880), 171.

3   A. Donald MacLeod, *A Kirk Disrupted: Charles Cowan MP and the Free Church of Scotland* (Fearn Ross-Shire: Christian Focus, 2013), 39.

4   Hugh Miller, "The Disruption", in *Headship of Christ and the Rights of the Christian People* (Boston: Gould and Lincoln, 1863), 478–479.

5   Hanna, *Memoirs of the Life and Writings of Thomas Chalmers*, 2:645–646.

6   Ibid., 647.

Chapter 9

1   Quoted in John Roxborogh, *Thomas Chalmers Enthusiast for Mission*, 155.

2   Hanna, *Memoirs of the Life and Writings of Thomas Chalmers*, 2:671.

3   Thomas Chalmers, "Dr. Chalmers' Essay," in *Essays on Christian Union* (London: Hamilton & Adams, 1845), 16–17.

4   Hanna, *Memoirs of the Life and Writings of Thomas Chalmers*, 2:728–729.

5   Ibid., 2:750.

6   Ibid., 2:751.

7   Hanna, *Memoirs of the Life and Writings of Thomas Chalmers*, 1:458.

8   William King, *Autobiography of Rev. William King: Written at Intervals During the Last Three Years of His life* (Typescript n.d., Presbyterian Church of Canada Archives), 171–172.

9   John Anderson, *Reminiscences of Thomas Chalmers, D.D. LL.D* (Edinburgh: James Nichol, 1851), 371.

10 Thomas Chalmers, *The North British Review*. 7 (May–Aug. 1847), 261–262.

11 Hanna, *Memoirs of the Life and Writings of Thomas Chalmers*, 2:780.

Chapter 10

1   Hughes Oliphant Old, *The Reading and Preaching of the Scriptures in the Worship of the Christian Church*, vol. 2, *Moderatism, Pietism and Awakening* (Grand Rapids MI: Eerdmans, 2004), 513.

2   Hanna, *Memoirs of the Life and Writings of Thomas Chalmers*, 1:304.

3   Thomas Chalmers, "Courteousness," in *Sermons by the Late Thomas Chalmers D.D., L.L. D., Illustrative of Different Stages in his Ministry, 1798–1847* (New York: Harper & Brothers, 1849), 70.

4   Ibid., 76.

5   Ibid., 89–91.

6   Hanna, *Memoirs of the Life and Writings of Thomas Chalmers*, 1:317–318.

7   Ibid., 318.

8   Ibid.

9   Thomas Chalmers, *Sermons, Preached in the Tron Church Glasgow by Thomas Chalmers, D.D. Minister of the Tron Church, Glasgow* (Glasgow: John Smith and Son, 1819).

10 Ibid., 209–210.

11 When these were published in Chalmers' Complete Works, he stated that his original sermons preached at St. John's "extend only a little way into the tenth chapter, and that the remaining lectures, with the exception of the one on xiv. 17, have been only prepared now for the completion of this work."

12 Thomas Chalmers, *Lectures on the Epistle of Paul the Apostle to the Romans* (Glasgow: William Collins, 1837) 1:340–341.

13 Thomas Chalmers, *Lectures on the Epistle of Paul the Apostle to the Romans* (Glasgow: William Collins, 1840), 3: 403.

14 For a summary and biblical defense of post-millennialism see, John Jefferson
    Davis, *Christ's Victorious Kingdom* (Laurel, MS: Audubon Press, 2006).

15 For a summary of the historical background on the Scottish understanding
    of eschatology see, Alasdair Black, "The Balfour Declaration: Scottish
    Presbyterian Eschatology and British Policy Toward Palestine," *Perichoresis*,
    vol. 16 no. 4 (2018), 35–59.

16 Thomas Chalmers, *Lectures on the Epistle of Paul the Apostle to the Romans*
    (Glasgow: William Collins, 1840), 4:184.

17 Ibid., 4:187.

18 Thomas Chalmers, "The Expulsive Power of a New Affection," in *Sermons
    and Discourses of Thomas Chalmers*, 2:273.

19 Ibid., 274.

20 Ibid.

21 Thomas Chalmers, "Importance of Civil Government," in *Sermons and
    Discourses of Thomas Chalmers*, 1:345.

22 Ibid., 351.

23 Thomas Chalmers, "On Cruelty to Animals," in *Sermons and Discourses of
    Thomas Chalmers*, 2:260.

24 Hanna, *Memoirs of the Life and Writings of Thomas Chalmers*, 1:445.

25 Ibid., 445–446.

26 Thomas Chalmers, "Principal's Address, November 1845," in *Prelictions
    on Butler's Analogy, Paley's Evidences of Christianity, and Hill's Lectures in
    Divinity* (Edinburgh: Thomas Constable and Co, 1852), 469.

27 Quoted in Michael J. Ives, "Desert Rose, Thomas Chalmers' West Port
    Experiment (1844–1847)," *The Confessional Presbyterian* 14 (2018), 125.

Chapter 11

1   "Thomas Chalmers," *The Spectator* no. 988, (June 7, 1847) accessed April 24, 2019, http://archive.spectator.co.uk/article/5th-june-1847/11/it-is-not-often-that-a-man-can-be-said.

2   Ibid.

3   McCaffrey, "Thomas Chalmers and Social Change", 34.

4   McCaffrey, 45.

5   Donald Macleod, "The Establishment Principle Today" accessed June 7, 2019, https://donald macleod.org.uk/dm/the-establishment-principle-today.

6   Ibid.

7   Ibid.

8   Ibid.

9   Stewart J. Brown, *Thomas Chalmers and the Godly Commonwealth* (Oxford: Oxford University Press, 1982), 378. Although I have arrived at different conclusions with respect to Chalmers' legacy, Brown's richly detailed biography is an indispensable aide to those who want to know about Thomas Chalmers.

10 Michael Fry, *A New Race of Men: Scotland 1815–1914* (Edinburgh: Birlinn, 2013), 176.

11 Thomas Chalmers, "On the Advantages of Christian Knowledge to the Lower Orders of Society," in *Sermons and Discourses of Thomas Chalmers*, 2:343–344.

Index

Scripture